How to Build and Manage a

Family Law Practice

by Mark A. Chinn

SECTION OF FAMILY LAW
LAW PRACTICE MANAGEMENT SECTION

Cover design by Gail Patejunas.

10 09 08 07 06 5 4 3 2 1

Library of Congress Cataloging-in-Publication Data

Chinn, Mark A.
    How to build and manage a family law practice / by Mark A. Chinn.
      p. cm. — (Practice-building series)
    Includes index.
    ISBN 1-59031-695-9
    1. Practice of law—United States. 2. Domestic relations—United States. I. American Bar Association. Section of Law Practice Management. II. Title. III. Series: Practice-building series (American Bar Assocation. Section of Law Practice Management)
    KF300.C455 2006
    340.023'73—dc22   2006042786

Contents

CHAPTER 3
Mission and Goals   13

CHAPTER 4
Start-Up   21

CHAPTER 5
Systems   27

CHAPTER 6
Marketing   35

CHAPTER 7
Intake of the New Client   57

CHAPTER 8
Fees and Billing   67

CHAPTER 12
Service   131

CHAPTER 15
Getting to Court   175

CHAPTER 16
Case Management   183

CHAPTER 17
Time Management   187

CHAPTER 18
Financial Management 197

CHAPTER 19
Getting Better
207

CHAPTER 20
Taking Care of Yourself
213

CHAPTER 21
Parting Thoughts   221

About the Author

Mark Chinn has specialized in family law for the last twenty-four years of his twenty-eight years of practice and operates a family law firm in Jackson, Mississippi, along with four other lawyers. Mark is a longtime member of the ABA Section of Family Law and currently serves as a member of its governing council and publications board. He is listed in *The Best Lawyers in America*, Martindale-Hubbell's *Bar Register of Preeminent Lawyers* in the field of family law, *America's Registry of Outstanding Professionals*, and the *Metropolitan Executive and Professional Registry*. He is one of the one hundred attorneys selected in the state of Mississippi for membership into the *Outstanding Lawyers of America*. He has an AV rating and is certified in Civil Trial Advocacy by the National Board of Trial Advocacy. He is also listed in *Who's Who* and *Who's Who in American Law*.

Mark is a contributing author of *How to Capture and Keep Clients*, a publication of the GP Solo Practice Management Section of the ABA, and *101 Practical Solutions for the Family Lawyer*, a publication of the ABA's Section of Family Law. He has been a frequent speaker for the ABA Section of Family Law and the Mississippi Bar on law practice management and client relations.

Mark was the recipient of the Award of Merit for distinguished service to the bar and the public in 1996 and was enrolled as a fellow of the Mississippi Bar Foundation in 1997. He has been chairman of the Section of Family Law of the Mississippi Bar twice. His work with the Mississippi Bar has included chairman in 1995–1996 of the Solo and Small Firm Practice Committee, and past service on the Ethics, Client Relations, Women in the Profession, and Fee Dispute Resolution committees.

Mark was chairman of the Lamar Order of the Alumni Association of the University of Mississippi School of Law in 2002. He was president of the Hinds County Bar Association in 1998–1999 and is a master of the bench in the Charles Clark American Inn of Court. He was vice chair of the Mississippi Supreme Court's Gender Fairness Task Force and was appointed by the governor of Mississippi to the Children's Justice Task Force. Community activities include chairman of the Jackson Urban League Board of Directors (1995–2000); chairman of the Tenth Jubilee! Jam in May 1996, which featured the Olympic Torch; Jubilee! Jam Foundation Board; Arts Alliance Board; Opera Board; and Leadership Jackson.

Mark also lectures at the Ole Miss Law School and has been an adjunct professor of law at the Mississippi College School of Law, where he taught a course he designed in Law Practice Management. He received his undergraduate degree from Iowa State University in 1975 and his law degree from the University of Mississippi in 1978. He is admitted to practice in all courts in Mississippi, the Courts of Appeals for the Fifth and Seventh Circuits, and the United States Supreme Court.

Mark is married to Cathy, and they have four daughters, Courtney, 22, Casey, 15, Carly, 10, and Conley, 7.

Acknowledgments

I wish to thank the ABA Section of Family Law Publications Board, chair, Linda Ravdin, and the Law Practice Management Section of the ABA, for giving me the opportunity to write this book.

In addition, I extend my appreciation to: Jerry Schwartz of Legal Management Services in Memphis Tennessee, who has been my law firm management consultant and confidant since 1989.

Atticus law office management consultants of Orlando, Florida, and my personal coaches, Mark Powers and Shawn McNalis, who have helped me to improve not only my practice but my life.

The University of Mississippi Law School, which gave me the education and training that would allow the life I have so deeply enjoyed.

The Team at Chinn & Associates, Chad, Patricia, Judy, Dar Kenya, Mary Anne, Peggy, Lee Ann, Drew, Matthew, and Bo, who have helped create a culture of excellence and friendship and service.

Linda Harper, who was my teammate in building my practice and sacrificed so much.

Honorable Carroll Ingram, Hattiesburg, Mississippi, my mentor and friend, and Honorable Tom Crockett, Jr., Jackson, Mississippi, my "civility coach."

And my wife, Cathy, and our daughters, Courtney, Casey, Carly, and Conley Chinn.

Preface

This book provides a guide to building or refining a family law practice, which represents one of the most unique and challenging specialties in law. It packs a *triple punch* from the standpoint of challenge: family lawyers must be accomplished litigators; they must understand law and procedure; and they must approach every case as though it were going to trial someday.

Family law combines litigation with accounting and psychology. Accounting plays a role in the vast majority of cases. Family lawyers are called upon to review budgets and financial statements and analyze tax returns. They are also called upon to orchestrate a legal audit of companies and personal spending practices, as well as advise clients in financial planning.

Family lawyers must also be psychologists. Family law cases are typically packed with the most extreme of family emotions. The family lawyer must understand the psychology at work in the marriage or in the parenting of children as well as negotiate the treacherous slope of working with clients in extreme emotional pain. Indeed, the family lawyer must find a way to coach people through the worst time of their lives.

The lawyers who turn to family law are those who have the aptitude to understand finances and the interest in people to understand their workings, all while remaining the most astute of litigators. Lawyers who devote themselves to family law can be called the gladiators of the human condition. While the work is most challenging, the professional satisfaction is most profound. No family lawyer will ever forget the hug he or she receives from the client to whom custody of children has been restored. No lawyer will ever enjoy a greater accolade than when a former client introduces you and says, "This is my lawyer. He is my hero because he got my baby back for me." No other lawyer will enjoy any greater satisfaction than successfully cross examining an adverse custody expert. No lawyer will enjoy any greater satisfaction than having a man say thank you for guiding him on how to save his marriage and family. Family lawyers know what it means to level the playing field for a victim of marital abuse and set her free to enjoy an empowered life. Family lawyers, perhaps more than any other specialty, work in the trenches of the lives of their clients. More than any other occupation, family lawyers change lives for the better in the face of adversity.

Since the practice of family law, by combining litigation and the emotion of family issues, may be the most emotionally draining specialty in law, family lawyers face serious life management issues. They are challenged to manage their own emotions and the tremendous drain on their energy. For these and other reasons, family lawyers must learn to lead healthy lives or fall victim to hypertension, heart attack, back and neck problems, chemical abuse, and family strife.

This book is written for lawyers at every level of experience who are thinking about starting their own business and specializing in family law.

Why would one want to build and manage a practice specializing in family law?

Creating your own business creates freedom—

To come and go as you please
To create a practice that fits your vision
To live your own lifestyle
To hire and fire your own staff
To create spinoff businesses and ventures
To create perks from the practice

Creating a specialized practice—

Allows you to refine your skills
Permits you to work in familiar territory
Enhances your professional representation
Sets you apart from the masses of lawyers
Provides a good living

This book is dedicated to building and managing a family law practice. It covers topics similar to those in other books on how to start law practices, but the tone, tenor, and content focus on the family law practice. It also presents some discussions that cannot be found in other law practice management books.

I will walk you through the mental and spiritual steps to help you build the courage to go out on your own. I will discuss the mechanics of opening your own office, marketing, hiring and firing staff, dealing with adversity, service, billing and collecting fees, and fiscal management, to name a few. In addition, systems, procedures, protocols, and checklists are discussed throughout the book, and the compact disc that accompanies the book contains extensive appendices. See page 237 for a list of the Appendices referenced throughout this book.

Introduction

I can remember fellow members of the bar telling me in the early years of my career, "Chinn, when are you going to go out on your own?" I would reply, "I don't think I could take that risk." They would say, "Come on, you gotta jump into the deep end." Well, I played it safe for years, practicing under other peoples' direction for ten years. And then it became crystal clear to me that no matter how well I performed or how dutiful I might be to my employer, I was never going to get from other people what I wanted. I knew that I had no choice but to start my own practice. I was at the point where the prospect of failure or bankruptcy did not matter.

So, I began to plan. I knew I had to prepare, but more than that, I knew I had to move fast. I made a list of supplies and went to the local office supply store where I spent $115 for legal pads, pens, copy paper, paper clips, staplers, file folders, fasteners, and hole punchers. I talked to a friend who had some extra space and arranged to sublease from him. In a stroke of luck, the previous occupant of the office space had elected to retire and wanted me to look after her furniture. She had two old-fashioned red phones with two lines. I called the phone company for a phone number and decided to keep the two lines. Even though the need for two lines at that time was laughable at best, I figured the worst thing possible was for a potential client to be unable to get a hold of me because of a busy line. I picked a phone number that spelled

"ATTY." I thought that was catchy. I went to the post office and got a post office box.

Next I went to the bank and announced that I was starting a business. I asked the bank to advise me on what types of accounts and checks I needed. I opened two accounts, one for "operating" and one for trust. I got a large three-ring checkbook for each account. I thought that looked more businesslike than a simple checkbook.

In just a few short days, I had arranged for my office, my furniture, my mail, and my phones; I was ready to move. I opened my office on July 1, 1988. I will never forget getting up early that morning to make sure I was at the office by 8:00, even though I had no business. I put on my best three-piece suit, even though I had no appointments. I went by the post office box shortly after eight that morning, even though there could not have been any mail there. I got started and I never looked back. I made as much money in the next five months as I would have made in a year with my employer. People came out of the woodwork to help me by sending referrals. Everything was lucky. Life has never been sweeter than the last seventeen years of practice on my own. Sure, being on your own brings challenges, but there is nothing like freedom!

As I struggled to run my practice, I became obsessed with reading and learning everything I could about personal and business management, especially law practice management. I sought coaching from several different sources and have continued with those coaches for years. Over the years I have spoken to lawyers all over the state of Mississippi on law practice management at the request of the Mississippi Bar. I have enjoyed making presentations for the ABA Section of Family Law throughout the United States and Canada. I served for five years as an adjunct professor of law at the Mississippi College School where I designed a course in law practice management. This book is the product of that experience and learning.

Jumping into the Deep End | **1**

IT IS NORMAL TO FEAR starting your own practice or specializing in a certain field, for both pursuits carry risk. Starting your own practice and specializing at the same time may be a little too much risk all at one time, unless you have a well-established reputation or are independently wealthy.

Fear is the biggest obstacle to success in any enterprise. It is the biggest obstacle to lawyers contemplating starting their own business or specializing. Fear can be a healthy warning sign, but usually it is a nonproductive, negative, paralyzing force. I am sure you have heard the saying, "Fear is false evidence appearing real."

You have all the training, skill, discipline, and drive that it takes to start your own business. Stop kidding yourself and look at what is driving your fear. Ask yourself, "What is the worst thing that would happen if I started my own business?" You may not make as much money as you thought you needed, and after some months you may decide to discontinue the effort. But you will still be a lawyer. You still have the ability to catch on with a firm and earn a living. The worst thing that would happen might be the debt you incur from the experiment, but that would simply be the fee you have to pay for the experience.

Develop Faith

Many people freeze up at the thought that they have no guarantees of sufficient business to make the leap. Certainly, that is a
concern in some situations, such as for a person right out of law
school or a person who has no history with family law. Otherwise,
any lawyer who is deterred from starting a family law practice
they want to start because they believe they need a guarantee of
sufficient business is failing to see the number one principle of life:
in life there are no guarantees.

Think about how many established, major corporations have
failed in the last year, businesses whose success you might have
viewed as guaranteed. Even McDonald's has experienced sales
downturns from time to time and must scramble to keep business
flowing. The answer is that any business must operate on faith—
faith that the universal forces will send business month in and
month out.

In his book, *How to Get Rich*, Donald Trump has this to say
about faith:

> I can remember a time when I had a choice to make, when I was
> billions of dollars in debt. I had to take one of two courses of
> action: a fearful, defensive one or a faithful, riskier one. I care-
> fully analyzed the situation, realized what was causing the
> uneasy feeling of fear, and immediately replaced it with blind
> faith, simply because I had nothing else to go on at the time.
> Then I resolved that as long as I remained disciplined, things
> would work out.[1]

Several years ago, I made the decision to elevate my practice
level. After consulting with several members of the ABA Section of
Family Law, as well as my personal coaches, I increased my hourly
rate, raised my retainer, and established a threshold for the type
of case I would accept. I boxed up my corporate notebooks and
sent them back to established clients and said, "Sorry, I am no
longer doing this kind of work." I made the commitment to refer
personal injury and other business—no matter how good—to
other lawyers. I am sure you can imagine the fear I had about

destroying the perfectly good business I had developed over the previous ten years. But I knew I had studied the situation and had sought good advice. And I knew I felt the calling to create a truly special practice. So, I went forward on faith. The point of recounting this story is that there are times in your practice when you must take risks if you want to improve your business. I am not telling everyone to throw out perfectly good business for no reason.

On the second day of the plan, I had a new client interview with a local businessman. I really wanted his business. When the time came to tell him my retainer, the blood seemingly drained from my body and I flinched, but an inner voice commanded, "Do it!" My consciousness ascended over my body and I watched, almost as a third-party observer, as my mouth opened and I said, "We ["we" being "me" of course], require a large retainer." I was sure he could see me cringing as the words left my mouth. Instead, he pulled out his checkbook and said, "I expected that," and then he continued, "Who do I make the check out to?" With the increased retainers, I opened two more files *that week*.

The decision to increase your business profile is a difficult one and should come only with careful examination and thought. It should be done for the purpose of improving the overall service of your firm to all of your clients by providing you with the means to meet their expectations.

Release the Result and Stay in the Moment

Any sports enthusiast knows that an athlete cannot perform if he is worried about the result. For example, any golfer knows that the worst thing to do is to have the final score in mind at any time during the round; this is true whether one is playing well or poorly. Contemplating the final score destroys the ability to perform properly on the shot at hand. My golf pro used to tell me, "Hit it and forget it." This applied whether the shot was good or bad.

Similarly, any musician knows that fear will choke the performance if the performer concentrates on anything other than the next note. Any tennis player knows that fear that a shot will go out is the surest way to yank it over the line. So release the fear about the result and take it one step at a time.

Coach Yourself

When you make a significant move in your life, you must coach yourself. You must remain positive. You must use every technique available to buoy yourself. When I started my own practice in 1988, I wrote an inspirational message on a note card and put it in my pocket. Whenever I felt a tinge of fear, I would pull the card out and speak the reaffirming quote out loud.

Use only positive language in your speech, even to yourself. Your brain is a computer that accepts programming from what it hears from your mouth. Do not use negative language or generalizations. Do not allow yourself even to say "this is a bad day." It will cast your brain's thoughts (program) in the negative. Instead, say, something like "I have had some challenging things happen today."

Act Deliberately and Quickly

Once you have decided to make a move in life, such as starting your own family law practice, keep in mind that delay and indecision are your enemy. Take action. Investigate. Research. Arrange. Do it now! Delay destroys confidence, allowing obstacles to form. Speak to few people about it. Of course, the caveat is to not act so quickly that you will be unprepared.

Read Jay Foonberg's Book

Jay Foonberg is a lawyer in California who wrote a book for the ABA Section of Law Practice Management called *How to Start and Build a Law Practice*.[2] This book is written in a conversational way and contains the information needed to start any law practice.

Notes

1. Trump, Donald, *How to Get Rich*, p. 72 (New York: Random House, 2004).

2. Foonberg, Jay G., *How to Start and Build a Law Practice*, Fifth Edition (Chicago: American Bar Association, 2004).

Tailor the Advice to Where You Are 2

THE ADVICE IN THIS BOOK does not necessarily apply across the board to all lawyers at all levels. Lawyers at differing levels of experience, expertise, wealth, and position must carefully assess where they are in the scheme of things and apply the advice in this book carefully. The rules must change and bend depending on your situation.

A Brand New Start

If you are a brand new lawyer, special considerations apply. Think of it: You have no experience, no track record, no client list, no referral sources. You may have few financial resources. Starting a new practice is a very risky proposition. And if you plan to start a specialized practice, the risk increases exponentially. That does not mean it cannot be done, but realize that it will be very difficult.

If you want to enter practice on your own right out of law school, realize that you are a special individual and that you will need special circumstances. Listed below are some of the qualities and circumstances that might lend themselves to such a bold move.

Your Spouse Is a Doctor

One way to open a practice on your own right out of law school is to marry a doctor. Tongue in cheek aside, it is true that one of the best ways to open a practice is to have no need for immediate money. This principle applies to people who have some independent wealth or to those who have a spouse who can support the family. Having some money allows you to take the time necessary to develop the skills, referral sources, and client base necessary to sustain a practice.

You Live in a Small Town

You were born and raised in a town of 10,000 or less and you went to your state's law school. In such a scenario, a lot of people in both your town and county know you and will be happy to help you with referrals. You likely also have contacts from the state or local law school, and local attorneys will feel comfortable sending you business because they know you well.

Your Parents or Grandparents Were Lawyers in the Same Community

Without question, people can benefit from an influential heritage, so if your father or mother had a strong practice in your community, that can get you started in your own practice. People will associate you with your relatives, and your relatives' friends will send you business. But keep in mind that it is up to you to merit the benefit of your birthright.

Share Space with an Established Lawyer

Sharing space with an established lawyer is the best way to open your own practice when you are a brand-new lawyer or are starting out on your own for the first time. The established lawyer will provide you with space, staff support, and equipment at less than what you could afford yourself. In turn, you can help the established lawyer to cut his expenses. And if you are truly compatible, he will be glad to serve as a mentor and send you business.

Advertising

Advertising allows brand-new lawyers to do what might have been unheard of otherwise: effective advertising can create name recognition that formerly took a lifetime to create. However, advertising cannot create anyone's professional reputation overnight, nor will it lead to a high-fee-paying clientele.

Advertising will be discussed in more detail later in the book, but suffice it to say here that the best forms of advertising for new lawyers are the following: radio, such as talk radio; the yellow pages; and free distribution newspapers. One of the lessons of law practice and life, however, is that every sword has two edges. With advertising, the good edge is that you will receive immediate recognition and new client calls. The bad edge is that you may be deluged with calls, most of which are not profitable business. The result may be increased overhead in screening calls and receivable problems. Another side effect is that you may be branded as a "low-cost lawyer."

First impressions are important and hard to change. Finally, another side effect of trying to appeal to the masses is increased exposure to liability and ethics complaints.

Do Not Partner with Other New Lawyers!!

One of the biggest mistakes law school or childhood buddies make is to think it would be cool to form a partnership right out of law school. Such a partnership is almost always a disaster. You never know a person—even if he or she is a close friend—until you try to do business together. What you find out is so often adverse. When you merge two or more people who have nothing, you still have nothing.

Specializing an Established Practice

Any law practice management specialist or coach will tell you that the secret to success is specialization. Thomas Stanley in *The Millionaire Next Door* believes that attorneys who specialize should be in great demand during the next twenty years and should have a profession that will lead to wealth.[1]

Mastering Your Trade

It takes ten years of sacrifice and work to master your trade, whether it be law, medicine, ministry, real estate development, interior design, landscape architecture, or any other line of work. If you have less than ten years of experience in family law, you must understand this rule and commit yourself to mastery. You must sacrifice to master your trade. Until you have done that, you may perform satisfactorily, but you are not a *master*.

Leaving a Firm

One of the surest bets for starting a practice is to join a firm that specializes in that practice. After working with them and developing skills, referral sources, contacts, and a client base, you may be in a good position to start your own practice. If you are going to pursue this course, make sure you select your firm carefully. You will be branded with their image for a long time, if not forever. You will learn from them. Your methods as well as your contacts, experts, and connections will come from them. Perhaps even more significant, your association with that firm will shape your personality and ways of doing things.

Success Stories

Gregg Hermann, Milwaukee, Wisconsin
In 1984, after serving seven years as an assistant district attorney, I received a message that a lawyer named Leonard Loeb had called

and wanted to talk to me about leaving the D.A.'s office and joining his family law firm as an associate. Me, a divorce lawyer? No way! I was in the middle of a first degree murder trial and was very much enjoying my work as a prosecutor. I threw the call slip away.

Late that afternoon, just before the jury went out to deliberate, the judge ordered the attorneys to a sidebar. With the jury having no idea what was being discussed, the judge ordered me and the public defender to join him for a beer immediately after the jury was charged. The judge emphasized: "This is not a request; this is an order. Now, do not smile or otherwise respond to me, but go back to counsel table and meet me in fifteen minutes." At the tavern, the judge told us what a fine job we had done on the case and how much he appreciated watching two fine lawyers at work. However, he urged us to move on because, as he said, we would soon be "institutionalized" and no firm would touch us. When I went back to my office, I dug Leonard's card out of the waste basket and called him the next morning.

While I was very impressed with Leonard and his practice, being a divorce lawyer still did not appeal to me. I turned down his job offer. In what Leonard later claimed to be a moment of temporary insanity, he asked to talk to me one more time. In that meeting, he essentially said the same thing the judge had said—that at a certain point no private firm would want an "institutionalized" lawyer. Still uncertain about being a divorce lawyer, I asked the district attorney for a one-year leave of absence so that I could "test the waters." For the first year of my practice, I thought every day of calling the D.A. and asking to come back! But believing that you either move forward in life or you move backward, I never made the call.

Fast forward twenty years. Having had the advantage of coming into an established practice, I had a ready supply of clients waiting for me. I was given time to develop my own practice. Eventually, Leonard and I became partners. When Leonard retired, I took over the practice entirely and now I have two associates. I try to give them the same advantages that I had initially—"hand-me-down" clients for now and time to develop their own practice for later. And the public defender? He is now a well-respected defense attorney and litigator in a prestigious private firm.

Jonathan R. Levine, Atlanta, Georgia

I developed my love for family law while working in a general business litigation firm. I handled some family law matters and learned that this area of law offered me the opportunity to interact directly with people. Each case had different fact patterns and legal issues. I left that general business litigation firm and worked as an associate for two years in a small family law boutique firm. After learning as much as I could and honing my skills, I opened my own practice. I started by sharing space in the back corner of a medium-sized law firm. Today I own a seven-member family law firm.

The most crucial ingredient of success in a family law practice is caring about your clients; if you care, it will show. A desire to serve each client to the best of your ability will be reflected in every aspect of your practice and will ultimately have a snowball effect on your ability to generate new business.

Note

1. Stanley, Thomas J., and William D. Danko, *The Millionaire Next Door*, p. 214 (Atlanta: Longstreet Press, 1996).

Mission and Goals 3

THE MOST IMPORTANT ASPECT of getting somewhere is knowing where you are going and when. It sounds trite, but it is the most important secret to success in any endeavor. In this chapter, we will explore mission statements and goal setting.

What Is Success?

You must define success in your life. If you are retired and are looking back, have you lived the way you should? What has that life looked like? What have you done professionally, financially, and spiritually? What type of family life have you had? What friends have you had? What principles have you followed? To know what success is, you must answer those questions; only then can you evaluate whether you are on the road to success.

Defining success involves a constant searching for direction in your life and making a continuous effort to follow that direction. Discovering your purpose and learning to pursue it is the key to true joy in life. One cannot experience that joy and meaning if you create a law practice that is not consistent with it. If the law practice does not serve the life you want to lead, there will be dissonance and strife in your life, and you will not succeed. Even if your practice is financially lucrative, you will experience other problems—marital unhappiness, loss of time with your children, or health problems. All things—work, home, and social life— are tied together. Therefore, you cannot start any practice without taking a complete inventory of your life and mission.

Stephen Covey in his book *The 7 Habits of Highly Effective People*[1] advises that "we must begin with the end in mind." Think about it. What builder starts a building without first obtaining detailed architectural plans? He will have a color picture of the final product; he will have detailed blueprints of the frame, electrical and plumbing connections and lines, and foundation. He will have target dates for beginning and ending the product.

At Yale, a study was done of graduates over a twenty-year period. At graduation, only 3 percent of the students had written life plans or goals. Twenty years later, it was found that the 3 percent that had written their goals had 97 percent of the wealth. Do you need any more evidence of Covey's position than that?

It Must Be in Writing

It has been said that the written word is the most powerful force in the world. When words are in writing, they serve as a visual command. In *The Game of Work*, Charles Coonradt stresses the necessity of written goals: "Writing goals allows us to transfer our dreams into a specific plan that can be handed to others to work on. Written goals are not opinions or whims or wishes. Writing goals is the key step that turns dreams into reality. It makes the difference between losing and winning."[2] Written goals are fixed and unchanged; they are not subject to differing recall.

A mission statement can be viewed as a personal constitution. Think about the Constitution of the United States. What value would it have if it were not in writing? It would have only the value that the most powerful man said it had, because he would be the one saying what it was. It would, therefore, guarantee rights to no one.

Writing Your Mission Statement

There are no set rules for developing a mission statement. It can be a narrative description of your life, it can be a listing of values and goals and ways of living and being, or it can be a series of "bullet points." If you don't have a particular way you want to write your statement, use the following guide:

Pick the things that are important to you and them rank them in order of importance. You can use the following list (or anything else you deem appropriate). Place a number of priority by each item, with "1" being the most important:

1	financial security	3 integrity
	extreme wealth	5 reputation
	material possessions	fun
	community	joy
4	family	hobbies
	marriage	relationships
	children	seeing the world
	professional standing	learning
6	physical health	adventure
	control of environment	fame
	creativity	politics
	friends	religion
	risk	advancement of a cause
	pursuit of talent	leading an authentic life
2	peace	living by chance
	spirituality	taking life as it comes
3.5	balance	music
	imbalance	art
	danger	sports
	power	developing your mind

When you pick what is important to you, you can then rank their importance. Here is my list, which you can use as an example:

1. Spirituality/God
2. Marriage
3. Children

ommunity/service

...mple of a Personal Mission Statement, see Appen-

...A.)

Goals

Success depends absolutely on creating definite goals. "Goal set-ting is the strongest force in the world for human motivation."[3] Success in life is equally enhanced by conceiving and writing goals. When I started my practice, I had one simple goal: to collect $10,000 per month. To my shock and amazement, I reached that goal in just my second year of private practice, in 1989. Shane Murphy's *The Achievement Zone* advises that you should "set goals that are just out of reach, but not out of sight."[4]

Goals Create Opportunity

Written goals are magical. I often tell people that if they write a goal down, it will happen! Writing them down opens our aware-ness of the people and circumstances necessary to achieve our goals, thus making them more likely to happen. Awareness is everything. Have you ever decided you liked a new type of car and thought to yourself, "you know, this car is new and there aren't very many on the road yet." And then, just as soon as you decide you like this type of car, you see it everywhere. Let's try this drill. Imagine that you are enamored of the new Volkswagen and want it in yellow. More than likely every other car you will see for the next several days will be a yellow VW! This same phenomenon of awareness works for us when we write our goals on paper. As Thom Hartman reports, "He who cherishes a beautiful vision, a lofty ideal in his heart, will one day realize it."[5]

(See Appendix 3B for a Personal Goal Setting Worksheet.)

Creating a Firm Mission and Goals

Just as you must have a personal mission, you must have a firm mission; all of the same principles apply. A firm mission statement stands as a beacon for all of your efforts, conveying who you are, what you are trying to accomplish, and how.

To be successful, we must design a business mission that is consistent with our personal mission: "If we set goals for ourselves that are not consistent with the purpose of our lives, then we'll find ourselves constantly frustrated, running up against the proverbial brick wall. We'll not succeed, or if we do, it will be a hollow victory."[6]

To design a firm mission statement, answer the following questions:

> What kind of business do I need to create to serve my personal mission and goals?
> What kind of work will the firm do?
> Who will the firm serve?
> What are the values of the firm?
> What level of technical skill will the firm strive for?
> What level of service will the firm deliver?
> What will make the firm unique or give it distinction?
> What geographic area will the firm serve?
> Does what I have created serve my life's purpose and goals?

Enlist help in creating your mission statement. If you have a supportive and trusted staff, schedule a firm retreat. You might even want to hire a facilitator. Such facilitators can be found both in private business and at local universities or community colleges. Get the whole staff away from the office and brainstorm about the firm mission and goals.

A firm mission statement should be short—as small as a paragraph—and it should be one that can be published to members of the firm, to clients, and to the public. Here is a mission statement sample:

> Our firm guides people through divorce where there are complicated legal and financial issues. We provide a unique staff, including lawyers, support staff, an accountant and a licensed professional counselor, with the goal of providing unparalleled service to our clients.

Your firm mission should be one that can be easily delivered to people when meeting them on social occasions. The statement should convey the *meaning* of what you do, instead of telling people *what* you do. For example, you are at a party and you are introduced to someone and he asks, "What do you do?" The common answer might be, "I am a divorce lawyer." Instead, you might answer, "I am a lawyer who guides people through family problems with a goal of securing the wealth they built during their marriage." For additional information, see Anthony Putnam's *Marketing Your Services*, Chapter 3.[7]

Chart the Future

Once you have developed a firm mission statement, take some time to envision the future. Project what you and and your firm will be like at key intervals in the future, such as five years or ten years from now. To help in this projection, answer the following questions for each year.

Describe who will be in the firm.
How many lawyers will there be?
What expertise will the lawyers have?
Will the firm be diverse?
Will the firm have different practice areas?
Will the firm expand to different cities or areas?
Will the firm build or will it buy a finished building?
What income will the firm or its members have?
What type of work environment will be created?
What hours will you be working, and what role will you
    perform?

(See Appendix 3C for a Firm Goals Worksheet.)

Notes

1. Covey, Stephen R., *The 7 Habits of Highly Effective People* (New York: Free Press, 1990).

2. Coonradt, Charles A., *The Game of Work*, p. 84 (Park City, UT: The Game of Work, 1991).

3. Ibid., p. 84.

4. Murphy, Shane, *The Achievement Zone*, p. 35 (New York: Berkley Books, 1996).

5. Allen, James, *As a Man Thinketh*, p. 42 (New York: de Vorss & Company, 1979).

6. Hartman, Thom, *Focus Your Energy*, pp. 68–69 (New York: Pocket Books, 1994).

7. Putman, Anthony O., *Marketing Your Services* (New York: John Wiley & Sons, 1990).

Start-Up 4

Select a Location Consistent with Your Personal Mission

GIVE CAREFUL THOUGHT to the location of your office. I have purposefully taken you through personal and business mission statements before discussing office location because you cannot make an educated selection without knowing what kind of personal life you want to lead and what kind of business you wish to serve. For example, if you decide that one of your personal missions in life is to be able to spend a lot of time snow skiing, you will make a huge mistake if you locate an office in the South. If you value the ocean, do not move to inland locations. If you value time with your family, seek a location close to your home. If you have child-care responsibilities, select a location close to your children's school.

Select a Location Consistent with Your Business Mission

One of the fundamental issues you need to settle when you are developing a business mission and plan is to determine *who* you want to serve. You should be able to provide a detailed description of what your clients will look like, their characteristics, their income levels, their trades, and the sources they will consult to select a lawyer. Once you can describe your prospective customer, you can then determine where they are and where they would feel most comfortable traveling to see you.

Let us look at an example. Suppose in starting your family law practice, you determine that your mission is to provide high-quality professional service to people seeking divorce for a fee that is slightly less than the highest level. You will cater to people who want a high level of service but who are looking for a bargain. You are not catering to the masses because you are charging a fairly higher fee. Therefore, you have no interest in being seen from the road or in being available for people who walk in off the street. Your business will come from solid referral sources who know you do good work but do not charge the highest fees. All of this means that your location does not have to have high visibility. On the other hand, you determine that most of your referral sources will be the lawyers who occupy the buildings downtown, so you feel it might be beneficial to be where those referral sources are so that you will be in their view on a daily basis. But knowing your clients will appreciate the difficulties that downtown parking can create, you look for a small "walk up parking" building that is very close to downtown but not in it. This will put you close to your referral sources but not in the thick of the city where your clients may not feel comfortable going.

Alternatively, you may decide that you want to offer basic discount services to the masses at a reduced rate. Your goal is to get as much business as possible and learn to serve it efficiently so that you can maximize profit from low fees. You determine that the people who will be served by this type of service will be located in blue-collar neighborhoods and so will be less likely to have access to the lawyers who occupy the downtown buildings. It appears that these potential clients will be more likely to come to you if you are visible from the road. So, you select a location in a blue-collar neighborhood on the main drag where everyone will see your name everyday on the way to work or to the store.

Your selection should also take the long term into consideration. For example, think about the places within the community that you might want to move in the future. Pick your first location in the same phone number district as these places. That way you will not have to change your phone number. Changing phone numbers, street addresses, and e-mail addresses can frustrate new business callers and impair profit.

Furniture

In the beginning, do not spend a lot of money on equipment and furniture. Avoid excessive debt or lease obligation when you are just starting out. When I opened my own practice in 1988, I was fortunate to find a friend who agreed to sublet space to me and share his reception room and receptionist. For this I got away with paying a modest monthly fee. By sheer good luck, the lawyer who was leaving the office was temporarily retiring and did not have anywhere to put her furniture and phones. It was very nice furniture, and she said I could use it if I would take care of it for her. If you are not so lucky, look for used furniture in the want ads or at fire sales. Furniture loses value the second you buy it, but it retains most of its appearance and use. As your practice matures, you can gradually add nicer furniture.

Phones

When you buy phones, you usually buy a telephone provider. Select your provider very carefully because you will be tied to it for awhile. You must obtain at least two phone lines, even if you are alone and have no business. The worst thing that can happen is for someone to call your office and receive a busy signal.

Be careful to make your move at a time that will make inclusion in the phone book possible. It could be a kiss of death to be in practice for a full year without a listing in the phone book.

Since the phone is the number one source of contact with your firm, you will want to select a phone number that is catchy or memorable. Everything about it should be easy for both new and existing customers. Your phone company representative can help you select a phone number that will facilitate people remembering your number without looking it up.

Equipment

Do not overload yourself with equipment when you start. When I started, I did not even buy a copier: I borrowed another lawyer's copy machine and paid him per page. It was not cost effective in the long run, but in the short run, it kept my capital investment low and controlled my costs by the case. Best of all, I was not tied to a lease payment. For his part, the other lawyer liked this arrangement because it helped him recover the cost of his machine.

When you are ready to get your own machines, ask the sales representative if they have any used equipment. They usually do, and the price is usually quite attractive for very nice machinery.

Leaving the Firm

If you are contemplating leaving a firm to start your own business, plan the move carefully but do not delay. This advice applies to almost any bold plan. In most cases, you should advise your employer before making a move away from the firm, for honesty and forthrightness are almost always best in the long term. If you handle it properly, the firm you leave could become one of your best referral sources in the future.

If you feel, however, that your employer will interfere with your move or prevent you from acquiring the business you are entitled to, then you may decide to make the move in secret. If this is the case, you must act fast. Some years ago, a small group of lawyers planned to leave a big firm, intent on a secretive move so that they could leave with some of the firm's business. Wanting to make sure they took care of every detail, they were quite deliberate in their planning. Unfortunately, they leased space on a different floor of the same building. About a week before their planned midnight departure, a phone company installer arrived at the old firm to ask where the new phones were to be installed. The plot was revealed, and alas, the boys had to move one week earlier than planned. (Jerry Schwartz of Legal Management Services in Memphis, Tennessee, has developed an office start-up time line and checklist, which is included as Appendix 4A.)

Systems 5

IN *RICH DAD, POOR DAD*, Robert T. Kiyosaki retells the answer his rich dad gave him to his question as to why McDonald's makes more money than everyone else when just about anybody can make a better hamburger: "The answer is obvious," he said. "McDonald's is excellent at business systems. The reason so many talented people are poor is because they focus on building a better hamburger and know little to nothing about business systems."[1]

By creating systems, you can develop a practice that will ultimately work without you. Michael Gerber warns that "[i]f your business depends on you, you don't own a business—you have a job. And it's the worst job in the world because you're working for a lunatic!"[2] Gerber believes the rule of creating systems applies to law firms:

> Obviously, if [your business] is a legal firm, you must have attorneys.... But you don't need to hire brilliant attorneys.... You need to create the very best system through which good attorneys ... can be leveraged to produce exquisite results. The question you need to keep asking yourself is: How can I give my customer the

results he wants systematically rather than personally. . . . How can I create a business whose results are *systems*-dependent rather than *people*-dependent?[3]

In *Fail-Safe Leadership*, Linda Martin emphasizes the role of systems in success: "Successful people are those who are effective at achieving desired outcomes because they follow a predetermined set of processes that LEAD to those outcomes."[4]

At every step of the way in your practice, you should be constantly developing systems, procedures, and checklists. Before you have employees to whom you can delegate duties, these systems, procedures, and checklists will help you deliver the same high product level, time and time again, with minimum effort. Once you have established yourself as a true master and technician of your trade, and have developed enough business to hire people, these systems, procedures, and checklists will help your employees deliver the same level of work you would deliver if you were doing it yourself. This will help you distribute work, take in more work, and "leverage" your business-getting ability to make profit.

In *The E-Myth Revisited*, Michael Gerber teaches that a successful business owner must have three personalities: that of the technician, the manager, and the entrepreneur. All good lawyers are good "technicians" and are masters of their trade. The same is true for most small-business owners, who often make the fatal assumption that since they understand the technical work of a business, they understand the business that does the technical work.[5] The problem is that successful business owners must know not only how to do the business, but also how to create (the entrepreneur) and manage business. Most lawyers abhor the thought of being entrepreneurs or managers. You will hear them say, "All I want to do is practice law." Refusing to train yourself to become an entrepreneur and manager will limit your success significantly, if not send you seeking a job for someone who has done it.

Here is how to create systems and procedures for your office:

1. Whenever you confront a problem, ask yourself the following questions: What is the problem? What causes it? What system can I put in place to make sure this does not happen again?

2.   Create a checklist for everything you do and then make sure the checklist is actually used, "checked off on," and placed in the file. I learned this technique while training for my pilot's license. Every flying procedure is broken down into steps and placed in a checklist, which pilots carry with them whenever they fly. No matter how experienced the pilot is, he or she will review the checklist for all procedures. When you board a plane, you will notice that the pilots are going through checklists in preparation for flight.

3.   Write scripts. If you want something handled in a certain way, write a script for it. This will help you analyze exactly why you want something handled a certain way. It will also help you improve it. The script will help you and staff handle things exactly the same way every time.

4.   Create and write policies. Create policies for everything you do. Communicate and re-communicate the policies again and again. "Some experts say that only after hearing a message six times does a person begin to believe and internalize."[6] You must reinforce your ideas daily in your interactions with all the people in your organization.[7]

5.   Train staff to follow policies and fire those who will not. Good employees want to know what you expect of them and are happier when they do. But all members of the team must be constantly reminded to follow the policies and procedures. If there is a need to deviate from these set policies, the rest of the team must be so informed and the appropriate superior must approve the change. For example, when a quarterback calls a play in the huddle, every player must run that play exactly as it was drawn up. If someone deviates, the outcome will be disaster. This does not mean that you do not want changes. If the quarterback sees the need to change the play, then he should, but he must let everyone else know by calling

an "audible." As Gerber says, "What you do in your model is not nearly as important as doing what you do the same way, each and every time."[8]

Those who do not understand the principle of following systems and procedures will argue that this is "micro managing." This is hogwash! The organization can function well only if all of the members of the team work together.

6. Create forms. Every time you write a letter or draft a pleading, draft it in a model form for use in the future. Write it in as generic a way as possible so that it can be used in almost any case with little change. For example, your letters should refer to a "spouse" as opposed to a "husband" or "wife." This will minimize the need for changes. Save these forms in a three-ring notebook, which is indexed, or in your Word Perfect system in a file called Forms. After a while, you should have prepared every type of letter or pleading that you will ever write, and so all you will have to do is reach for the proper form. There is a caveat to using forms, however: Be careful that the form is correct for the situation; do not just blindly use any kind of form. They are designed to increase efficiency, but they are not a substitute for thought.

Correspondence

All correspondence, notes, copies of phone notes, and e-mails should be bound in a hard cardboard folder, neatly and in chronological order. There should be nothing loose in the file; everything must be bound down. Something that is not bound down may fall out of the file and get lost, or may interfere with finding other materials. For example, if the client provides you with a small cassette tape of a conversation, place the tape in an envelope, label the envelope, and then bind the envelope down in a folder that is properly labeled. This ensures that the tape can be easily retrieved. An alternative to binding papers down in a folder is the use of a three-ring notebook.

Pleadings

Pleadings should be meticulously kept in folders or notebooks in chronological order, and then indexed and tabbed for easy location. Before going to court on any motion, have your staff make sure that all pleadings are in the index and are properly labeled. That way, you will not be missing a recent or critical pleading when arguing in court.

Sometimes there is a response to a document request or a subpoena that is voluminous and not susceptible to filing in the pleadings index. When that occurs, file a note in the pleadings index which says something like this: "Documents provided in response to subpoena are in a separate folder labeled, 'Documents Produced by State Bank.' "

Folders

Items that are not correspondence or pleadings should be stored in separate folders or notebooks that are properly labeled. For example, tax returns should be filed in a folder labeled "Tax Returns." Photos of bruises on the client should be placed in an envelope, which is bound down in a folder labeled "Photos of Bruises on Client."

Releasing Materials

At times a client will request return of a document, piece of evidence, or videotape. *Never* return a file item to clients without having them sign a receipt and placing the receipt in the file. They may well ask you for it later and then blame you for losing it when you cannot find it.

The File Must Tell a Story

The file must be maintained so that any member of the firm can pick it up at any time and tell exactly what has been happening. I started doing this when I was a solo practitioner because I soon realized that I could not remember everything. I needed to keep meticulous records for *me*. The need for this recordkeeping increases when more than one person is working on a file. Everyone who picks up the file must be able to tell what has gone on before; otherwise, client service is severely impeded.

Numbering

Number files by the year of their beginning and by the subject. For example, the first file opened in 2005 would be numbered 2005–001, or 05–001. This allows you to keep track of file-opening activity in any one year. The files can be shelved in numerical order. Use different colors of file folders for each year; this will provide a little differentiation to keep files from being misfiled. Maintain a Rolodex with file numbers saved by file name, kept in alphabetical order. Another option is to discard the Rolodex and store files in alphabetical order. If you use this method, use different file colors for different letters of the alphabet.

Research: Look at the Code First

I once had an associate who would answer my research questions with cases from other states and law journal citations. I would look at his memo and ask, "Did you look at our state code?" He would blink, squirm in his chair, and say, "I didn't know there was a code section on this." Frustrated, I would reply, "Well, the best reasoned law journal article in the world doesn't matter if there is a code section that covers this." And then I would say, "Never commence a research project without *first* looking at the code." There is an old saying in the South to beware of "the code lawyer." He does not seem smart or academic, and he has not looked at any law journal articles, but he has a code section that is going to be a stake in your heart.

Single-Case Method

One of the necessary traits of a great trial lawyer is simplification: judges need it, clients need it, you need it. Do not worry about finding all cases on a particular matter and analyzing them with law journal articles. One reason is that divorce court judges often do not have the desire or time to read them, nor do they have the staff to help them study them. Instead, find the one case that fits your case as closely as possible, take three copies of that case with you when you go to court, and highlight the pertinent language. When making your argument to the judge, state, "This case is covered by the case of *Jones v. Jones* which has similar facts to our case. There the court held in our favor on the issue presented here. Look at the highlighted quote on page 354, where the Supreme Court said, . . ."

Preserving Research

Trial lawyers do not have time to read briefs or memorandums. *They need the answer, and they need it quickly.* How do you do this? You get the pertinent cases—only a few—and put a yellow "stickie" on the front of the case, with a short statement of the holding and a reference to the page number which contains the key language. For example, a "stickie" might look like this:

> Commingling
> Separately held home ruled commingled by use as mari-
>   tal home
> See page 345 for ruling

Never allow anyone in your office to read a case without putting a stickie on the front of the case saying what it says in brief terms. If you do, then you will probably have to read the whole case again, *even if you were the one who read it in the first place!* The cases should be saved in a research folder or notebook.

Notes

1. Kiyosaki, Robert T., *Rich Dad, Poor Dad*, p. 126 (Paradise Valley, AZ: TechPress, 1997).

2. Gerber, Michael, E., *The E-Myth Revisited*, p. 40 (New York: Harper Collins, 1995).

3. Ibid., p. 100.

4. Martin, Linda L., *Fail-Safe Leadership*, p. 48 (Orlando, FL: Delta Books, 2001).

5. Gerber, *The E-Myth Revisited*, p. 13.

6. Lencioni, Patrick, *The Four Obsessions of an Extraordinary Executive*, p. 168 (San Francisco: Jossey-Bass, 2000).

7. Charan, Ram, and Noel M. Tichy, *Every Business Is a Growth Business*, p. 150 (New York: Random House, 1998).

8. Gerber, *The E-Myth Revisited*, p. 107.

Marketing 6

MANY LAWYERS VIEW MARKETING as either an unpleasant or an unprofessional task. However, if viewed from the proper perspective, marketing is neither. In fact, marketing can be rewarding and enhance professionalism. Other lawyers say they do not need marketing because they already have more work than they can handle. These lawyers are missing an opportunity to improve their practices and their lives.

Marketing can be fun. In its most basic format, it is nothing more than developing trusting referral relationships: friends. Now, unless you have an objection to creating positive, trusting relationships with as many people as possible, you can see that an effective marketing program will add to your personal life as well as your professional life.

The greatest threat to professionalism is a lawyer who is not making it financially. Lawyers who are struggling financially cut corners, provide inadequate representation, and "borrow" client funds. Therefore, it is critical to professionalism that lawyers have thriving businesses.

Finally, those lawyers who say they do not need marketing are missing the opportunity to improve their business. Effective marketing for the established lawyer can lead to higher hourly rates, more challenging or sophisticated clientele and business, and less labor for more dollars. Moreover, for the established lawyer marketing can ensure against downward cycles, which happen in all businesses.

Marketing Must Become a Way of Life

Marketing must become a part of your mentality and your daily life; it cannot be a one-shot thing. For example, I have worked out at the gym for many years. Every year after the new year has begun the gym is full of people who are fulfilling New Year's resolutions to get in shape. The regulars in the gym like to bet on how long the "New Year's Evers" will stay, whether it will be four or five weeks. As it turns out, most are gone by February. These "New Year's Evers" fail to realize that getting in shape is not a project, but a way of life. It is not a place to get; it is a process.

To effectively market, like the person who leads a healthy lifestyle you must develop the mentality that marketing is a way of life. For example, you cannot simply have an office party, send some letters, run an ad in the paper, and think this campaign will propel your practice to success. The office parties must be regular and identifiable, the letters must flow out of your office without interruption for your entire career, and the newspaper exposure must be relatively frequent. If you intend to use television, for example, you cannot decide to invest in TV advertising for six months and expect it to be enough. You must commit to long-term, unending advertising, or else all of the investment will be wasted. Just as fitness is a life-long commitment, so must marketing be a life-long endeavor.

Determining Your Target Audience

The most critical step in marketing is determining who you want to attract as referral sources and customers. This can only be done after creating personal and firm mission statements. The personal mission statement tells you what kind of life you want to have, whereas the firm mission statement must be structured to deliver the kind of life you want. Marketing must be designed to bring the firm the business it is designed to have.

Years ago, I contemplated using large yellow page advertising. A client of mine sold the advertising and worked hard to sell me on its benefits. She was able to quote statistics on the large number of calls that an ad would generate for me. She showed me impressive full-page ads she would like me to consider. The thought of receiving hundreds of calls for new business was quite alluring, but I thought I should investigate this change in my marketing direction very carefully. I decided to ask the opinion of people who sent me business and of the clients I most wanted to have. The key discussion took place with a local doctor who was clearly the type of client I wanted to continue to attract. He said, "I don't think you should do it. I don't want a lawyer who advertises (in the yellow pages)." That was all I needed to hear.

Let us be careful about what I am saying here. I am *not* saying a lawyer should not have a large, attractive yellow pages ad. As a matter of fact, such ads are wonderful for obtaining lots of a certain kind of business. The question is, will the ad (or any other marketing activity) yield the business you want? Mass advertising such as the yellow pages suggests this caveat: be prepared to have the staff and the phone lines to handle the calls, and be prepared to lose profitable billable hours screening the calls for paying business.

Profiling and Targeting Your Clients

To assist you in targeting your business, it is helpful to profile your prospective clients. What will they look like? The more detailed the description you have of your clients, the better your focus for your marketing efforts will be. Focus is necessary to prevent a waste of effort and money. For example, in the early years of my practice, I sought to profile my most preferred client.

Once you have described your ideal prospective clients, you must learn everything you can about them. For example, if you are targeting millionaires, you must research where they are, who they are, what they enjoy doing, what their hobbies are, and what type of medium or referral source they might use to find a lawyer. Read books such as *How to Meet the Rich*[1] and *The Millionaire Next Door.*[2]

A useful metaphor for understanding market targeting is fishing. You can have the best fishing boat on the ocean and the most sophisticated rods and reels and lures, and a great coastal fishing guide, but you will not catch a single thing in a lake where the bream will leap to a cricket at the end of a bobber and a cane pole. The point is, you must know your fish, their environment, and what they want to eat.

Profiling and Targeting Your Referral Sources

Most business for lawyers comes through referrals. Therefore, lawyers should not only market to potential clients, but must target and market referral sources. You should profile your referral sources. One way to do that is to examine the most profitable and rewarding cases you have already received. Where did those cases come from? Who sent them to you? Are there any consistencies there? For example, lawyers about your age in the big firms that do not handle divorce cases are a great referral source. Focus your efforts on those lawyers. Since you find such lawyers in bar associations, you should serve the bar as much as you can. This service is rewarding, allows you to give back to the public, and helps build relationships and name recognition with literally hundreds of lawyers who are potential referral sources.

Marketing 101

The Color of Their Eyes

Marketing is about building trusting relationships with people. The grass roots of marketing for the lawyer lies in every single personal contact. Whenever you are seen or interact with others, impressions are being created. First impressions are critical. In most interpersonal contact, the most critical element is *eye con-*

tact. It is my opinion that 99 percent of people never learn the wonderful art of total and concentrated eye contact with the people they meet. In seminars, I will ask the audience to turn and face another audience member and say "hello." Then, I ask them to cover their eyes and see if they can remember the color of the eyes of the person they have just met. Most often, they cannot. The reason: they have not truly focused on the individual in front of them, but only on the ceremony of the greeting. When you greet people, take time to learn the color of their eyes.

Use of the Business Card

The business card can be an extremely effective marketing tool, and it can also be meaningless. It all depends on how you use it.

Never, never, never, be without your business cards. Failure to have a card with you sends the signal that you do not take your profession seriously. Men should carry their cards in their shirt pocket. This allows for a "quick draw" of the card, which signals that your business is first on your mind. Women are less likely to wear shirts with pockets, so they might utilize a striking carrying case which they carry in their purse. In either case, the card should be easily accessed. Fumbling or searching for the card destroys the momentum of the marketing moment.

Presenting the Card

Jay Foonberg, author of *How to Start and Build a Law Practice*, teaches that the manner of presenting the card is critical.[3] He says that you should hold your card in both hands and present it as though it is a treasured gift. This communicates the idea that you treasure your profession and your business. Foonberg also states that you should *receive* a card from someone in the same way as you present your own—that is, with two hands, as though it is a treasured gift.[4] This makes the presenter remember you fondly as someone who respected them. And when you get the card, take it and look at it and comment on some favorable characteristic of the card. For example, if the person has placed a gold scales of justice on the card, you might say, "What a wonderful gold scales of justice on your card!" Again, this makes the other person feel good about himself, which makes him feel good about you.

Give people three cards instead of one. I learned this technique from a very successful personal injury lawyer in Alabama, who never uses either newspaper or television advertising but has a lot of good business. His technique was to give three business cards to every single person he meets, and even when he is in an elevator to people he does not know. There are several reasons for three cards. First, if you lose one, you will still have a card or two left. Second, the giving of three cards is special; with no one else doing it, it creates distinction. And third, the receiver is less likely to throw away three cards because it just seems too wasteful. So they are more likely to keep at least one.

Style

The style of the card should convey the message you want to send. It should speak to the people you want to reach, and it should be consistent with your stationery and all your other marketing efforts. For example, if you want to be perceived as bold and aggressive, but distinguished, you might choose a classic print with a little style but no flash. The card might be white and the print a rich, embossed black.

You can do many distinctive things with cards. You can put your picture on them, you can add a dash of color, you can add a word mark or symbol. Take the time to consider how your card should look. It is a basic marketing tool.

Stationery

The quality of the firm's stationery is a significant part of the firm's branding. For many firms and lawyers, stationery is the single most important marketing method. Consequently, significant thought should be given to the design, images, and paper quality. The stationery design should be consistent with all the firm's other communications. Many lawyers believe that significant thought and resources should be dedicated to selecting a fine quality paper.

For lawyers who are budget conscious, the ability to print your own stationery on your computer has reduced the need to obtain stationery from a printer. Many lawyers now utilize the computer to generate their own stationery.

The Next Level: Speaking and Writing

Speaking and writing are magnificent tools for developing lawyer referrals and for elevating professional standing. When you agree to speak for a continuing education program, for example, many marketing forces go to work for you. The first thing that happens is that you are listed on a program as a speaker. This creates the impression of expertise and excellence. Second, brochures advertising your name and the impression of expertise are mailed to every member of the bar to which the program is targeted. This places your name and purported expertise in front of literally thousands of your peers. Even if they are not interested in the seminar, they will likely open the brochure out of curiosity to see who is speaking before they throw it away. And, finally, if you are a good speaker, your audience will remember you not only as a competent and perhaps expert lawyer, but also as someone who took the time to help them become better. Often when I have been in jurisdictions in which I was not well known, I have had one or more lawyers come up to me and say, "You don't know me, but I heard you speak."

Writing, like speaking, reaches your audience and conveys an impression of expertise. There are many, many writing avenues available to you. For starters, your local or state family law section may have a periodical or newsletter. It may have a recent case discussion that you could author. In addition, state bars and CLE providers such as private companies and universities are always looking for authors. Call them and ask if they need an author.

You may choose to write an opinion or advice column in a local newspaper. You can call the newspaper and ask if it needs articles, or you could write an article and send it to the paper. Some small or local newspapers will accept just about any article, as long as you write it for them.

Bar Work

Your fellow members of the bar are responsible in large part for your professional reputation and standing and for sending you

business. You should take every opportunity to associate, socialize, and work with them. There is no better way to connect with
members of the bar than bar work.

Many lawyer ranking services base their rankings on the opinions of your fellow lawyers. Martindale-Hubbell Publishers provides one of the most prestigious ranking services. It ranks
lawyers in terms of ability and integrity. The highest rating is AV,
with the A standing for the highest ability ranking and the V for
the highest integrity ranking. This coveted ranking can only be
obtained from fellow lawyers. Obviously, professional standing
enhances business.

Lawyers are a leading source of referrals. Since most lawyers
do not advertise, the public usually asks for referrals from
trusted sources. People routinely ask their lawyer friends to refer
them to a lawyer who would be good for a certain type of case.
Moreover, most large firms do not handle family law, so when a
family law question comes up, they usually refer it to a family law
specialist.

There are many ways to serve the bar: through committee
work, section membership and work, and elective office. It is easy
to join a committee. All you need do is call the bar and ask for a
list of committees and join the committees that interest you. When
you serve on a committee and work on a project, the project—
though important—often becomes less important than the relationships you forge with other lawyers while working on it.

All state bars, most young lawyer associations, and many
local bars have sections. You should join the family law section of
every bar you can. You cannot consider yourself an expert in a
field if you are not a member of every available grouping of
experts in your field. Section membership involves a wide range of
activity, depending on the section. Most sections are relatively
inactive, with perhaps one meeting or CLE a year. Some, of course,
are more active. Make it a point to be involved as much as you
can. Other members of the bar have a sixth sense for your involvement. If they know you are at the heart of activity for your trade,
they will regard you as an expert worthy of referral. Moreover, you
will learn about your trade in your area. You will learn what the
other lawyers and judges are thinking and doing. You will also

develop relationships with them, which may enhance your dealings with them or may give you greater credibility in counties where you are not known.

Taking office with the bar is an excellent way to advance your reputation. There are countless positions, ranging from local bar directors to state bar representatives and local and state bar officerships. Usually, these positions are selected by nominating committees, and later they are submitted for vote. Find out when the nomination process takes place and who serves on the nominating committee and then solicit the nomination from the committee members. (Check your bar regulations on this before you do it, though.) If you are not nominated but still want the position, you can probably obtain candidacy through a petition process.

The ABA

Membership in the American Bar Association (ABA) practice sections and participation in their meetings and seminars bring many benefits. First, your ABA membership establishes you as a lawyer interested in learning and adhering to a national standard of professional development. Lawyers in your community and state will appreciate this and be more willing to make referrals to you. You will get many referrals each year from lawyers in your state where interstate issues are involved because they know you are involved in the ABA and have national contacts. (Lawyers from across the country and from foreign countries attend the ABA section meetings, so it should be relatively easy for you to establish yourself in your community as having these contacts.)

Second, you will make contacts with lawyers from around the country. Believe it or not, this can lead to business referrals. One of the best examples is a referral by a good friend of mine in the ABA of a professional athlete with a legal matter in Mississippi. Another benefit is the CLE and publications of the ABA. The ABA Section of Family Law publishes the *Family Law Quarterly*, which includes academic articles. It also publishes the *Family Advocate* magazine. Many issues of this magazine contain wonderful information for clients. These magazines can be given to clients for educational purposes. The Law Practice Management Section publishes articles and books on issues pertaining to managing the law practice and getting clients and delivering service.

Family Law Organizations

You can either join or seek induction into many organizations related to family law. Joining these state, national, or local groups of family lawyers has many benefits. First, it serves notice to the world that you are doing everything you can to enhance your professional skills by giving time and effort and money to meet with fellow family law lawyers to exchange information and ideas on improving your practice. Second, it creates professional contacts for potential referral. Finally, you will learn from the other members of the organization.

Awards and Honors

You will probably have the opportunity to apply for membership in "Who's Who"–type societies. These societies provide one more link, one more source for someone to see or get one's name, one more source of professional accreditation. There is usually an expense associated with these "honors," and you will just have to determine which ones, if any, you will choose to pay for.

Certificates

Some societies, such as the National Board of Trial Advocacy, test and certify lawyers for competence. It will give you confidence that a national organization has certified you as having special skills. The value of these certifications cannot be quantified, but you should seek every possible advantage to enhance your professional standing.

Community Work: Become a Pillar

Lawyers should be pillars in their community. First, service to the community is the right thing to do. From a practice management standpoint, however, it is an important thing to do. Lawyers are spokesmen or advocates for people, so that when a lawyer speaks for someone, he must be believed. People want to hire someone who will have credibility. They also want to hire someone who has good judgment. If people know that you are serving the community in a constructive way, they are more likely to perceive you as having judgment.

Finally, community service gets your name out to the public, which enhances your "top of mind awareness" for referrals. For example, for many years, I was involved with a festival in Jackson, Mississippi, called Jubilee! Jam. The city loves this event and flocks to it every year to listen to music of all kinds and party in the streets of downtown Jackson. My involvement with the "Jam" got me on TV many, many times. Reporters always covered the event and would interview volunteers (like me) who were organizing the event. I was also at the festival each year in my volunteer uniform, so my friends and acquaintances who came could see I was working for the community. And, of course, the countless hours of organizational work with literally thousands of volunteers, city officials, local businesspeople, and the media enhanced my name recognition and reputation in the community. Finally, it was fun!

Rotary, Chamber, and Other Community Organizations

Join community groups that have businesspeople as their members, and join as many as you can. Some examples of these groups are the Rotary Club, the Chamber of Commerce, the Optimist Club, and Junior League. Many of these business groups meet at lunch or breakfast. You can therefore invest in marketing without taking time away from your business or your home life. Most of these organizations are designed to create networking opportunities for their members.

Religious Affiliation

An essential part of being a pillar of your community is joining a religious organization, whether it be a church, synagogue, or mosque. Your congregation is a microcosm of your community, and many problems will arise among your members that will need your expertise. People will put more trust in you if they see you exercising your faith; they will be more likely to see you as someone who is stable and trustworthy.

Brochures

Brochures can be an important part of the total marketing package. A brochure should be carefully designed to give the prospective customer or referral source just the right amount of information in a fairly short amount of time and space. The brochure does not have to be in color, but it should probably have a good picture of you. The brochure should describe your firm mission, contain biographical information, and describe the service you provide. A brochure should not be long or detailed simply because most people today do not have the patience to read a lot of material.

If you have employees, do not include their picture in the brochure or even mention that you have any staff. They could leave the week after you pay for the brochures, and your brochure would be outdated immediately. You may be able to generate your brochure through desktop publishing. Just make sure the quality is good because, of course, you want to make a good impression.

Brochures can be distributed in many ways. You can pass them around to every member of any audience you speak to. You can carry brochures to bar or business meetings and hand them to people you meet. Or you can send them to prospective referral sources such as counselors, CPAs, or other lawyers.

People in the News

A great, hidden source of free mass marketing, known as People in the News, is that section of almost every newspaper that prints announcements such as hirings or promotions. Banks and insurance companies have discovered this wonderful source of free publicity, but lawyers seem to be oblivious to it. Use it to announce new hires, "promotions," and awards or honors. Simply write a sentence or two and send it to the paper(s) with a digital photo. Always include a photo because many people read only announcements that are accompanied by a photo. Keep a list of most, if not all, of the state's newspapers with names and addresses of the persons in charge of the People in the News. Keep a supply of photos to send.

Local Publications

Many publications are designed to reach people in places such as malls, bars, coffee shops, and other retail establishments. These publications are free to the public, and some develop almost cult-like followings. You should check out these publications in your area. Ask about the demographics of the readership, making sure that the demographics fit with your target audience.

Last year I started a mediation business called Divorce in a Day, which is designed to bring mediation services in divorce directly to the public. I advertised this new service in a local publication called *Coffee News*. *Coffee News* is one piece of paper printed on both sides, and each page is rimmed with two-by-two-inch ads. Only one of each kind of business is permitted. The middle of the *Coffee News* contains short stories and news items suitable for reading while one drinks a cup of coffee before work. Do not underestimate the value of this type of advertising. *The Millionaire Next Door* claims that millionaires like to go to coffee shops.[5]

Yellow Pages

The yellow pages is an effective place for almost any business to advertise. It is essential for any business to have a listing in the yellow pages because that is often where people who already know who you are will look for your phone number. To fail to have a listing could send the message of inattention to good business practices.

But the larger issues are how big and what kind of an ad you should have. To answer this question, you must first answer the threshold question of what kind of business you would like to have. If you wish to appeal to the masses, regardless of income, the yellow pages is a good choice. Lawyers who use large yellow page ads report that the ads work so well that they have to add phone lines and staff just to answer the calls. Not all of these calls, however, translate into paying business, moreover, they require many staff hours to screen the calls. If you wish to receive only calls from the type of person you want to represent, the yellow pages may be a disaster for you.

Television

Television can work for family law. Of course, this type of advertising is expensive—it is expensive to create the ads and expensive to run them.

The number one caveat for television advertising, as noted earlier, is to be prepared for a long-run commitment. I do not ever embark on this type of advertising unless I am prepared to advertise for an entire year, regardless of the success. Short-term television advertising is like pouring money down a drain. If you are thinking of television, talk carefully with the marketing representatives of each television station in your broadcast area. Analyze the demographics of each show to see how it compares with your desired client types.

Radio

Radio, perhaps the most overlooked form of advertising for lawyers, offers many ways to advertise. The obvious way is to create an ad and pay to have it run on a show. Production costs for a radio ad can be almost negligible. Moreover, the ad can consist of activities as simple as writing a script and visiting the station one day for a few minutes to record it.

Another way to advertise on radio is to appear as a guest on an existing show. If you want to be a guest, call some of the local AM talk shows and ask them if they are interested in having you discuss a topic of interest such as "How to Tell If Your Spouse Is Having an Affair." They may invite you as a guest (after you have already invited yourself). Or you may be able to purchase time as a "guest."

Yet another way to advertise on radio is to host your own show, perhaps a "call in" show on the issues of family law. Call your local stations and ask them how to do this.

Internet

Every reputable firm and every firm seeking to establish itself should endeavor to have a state-of-the-art web page. People are turning more and more to the Internet to find lawyers. The people using this resource are generally higher income, but the average income of Internet users is projected to decrease as computers spread through our society.

The key to successful Internet marketing is the search engine: You must be connected with a search engine that will lead to people finding your page. To check out how available your page is to the public, conduct your own search. Get on the web and type in some find words, such as "divorce" or "family law" in your state or town and see if you find your page.

Internet Marketing Companies

You will find that many companies will want to serve as a purveyor of your firm or web site on the Internet. These companies can lead to many referrals or to none at all. You must carefully investigate any commitment to an Internet purveyor to avoid wasting your money.

Use Pictures

All print or Internet advertising is enhanced by the use of a picture, so whenever possible, use a photo. If you advertise in the yellow pages, use a picture of yourself. If you send a note to People in the News, send a picture. Use pictures on your web page.

Contact Management Software

Periodic contact with people who might refer you business increases the likelihood of referrals. If you are on the "top of the mind" of a referral source, you have a better chance of getting the referral. How many times have you run into a friend who sent a piece of business elsewhere, either because she forgot what you do or she had not seen you in awhile? The best way to stay at the top of someone's mind is to make regular contact.

Contact management software makes periodic contact easy. This software can be used to automatically remind you to contact someone. You can program in birthdays, anniversaries, graduations, or regular periodic contact, such as every ninety days.

Many case management programs have this capacity built into the program. All persons whom your firm contacts, whether it be clients, attorneys, judges, referral sources, or court personnel, should be programmed into the system and categorized.

Ask every potential client who referred him or her to you and then place this name and contact information in the system as a referral source. The software allows you to select how often you wish to contact the referral source. You can send a letter or e-mail, and sometimes you can follow up with a call or lunch invitation. If the firm has been featured in an article or has received some distinction, you might send that to the referral sources. Send a picture of your children at an event or vacation. This personalizes the message and makes the referral source aware of the family they are helping with the income generated from referrals.

Here are two examples of the type of notes you can send to referral sources every ninety days or so.

> I was just up at the office this past weekend doing some thinking and planning for my divorce practice, and I thought of you and how much you had helped me with referrals in the past. I just want you to know how much I appreciate you for helping me.

> I just got back from the bar convention where my family won the sand castle building contest. Enclosed is a picture of my daughters and me in front of our prize-winning castle. Thanks for everything you have done for me in the past.

To make this activity less time consuming, write one generic note that can be used for several weeks for many people. When you mass produce letters, however, you should take care to make sure you do not send the same letter twice. You should also make sure the letter is appropriate for each person. There is a good chance that the receiver will know that you are mass producing contact letters, but, as long as you are careful with it, it will not diminish accomplishing the goal, which is "top-of-mind awareness."

You can make your contacts more personal, but keep in mind that it takes more time. Instead of mass producing letters, block out an hour or so of time each week to make personal calls. Another way to personalize your contact is to take post cards with you on flights or long car rides (with someone else driving of course!) and write personal notes.

A friend of mine who is a specialist in business valuation sends me cases, articles, or other material with his card stapled to it and a short personal note inscribed on the card, such as "Mark, thought you would benefit from this article." These short notes keep him in the top of my mind, and I usually benefit from the material he sends.

Saying Thank You

I refer many cases to lawyers every year, and it just amazes me how few send me a thank you. I would say that I get a thank you letter for maybe one out of every thirty referrals I make. I find that absolutely appalling. When you refer someone to a lawyer, it means that you are putting your own reputation on the line; that you are publicizing your belief that the person to whom you are referring is competent; that you are sending the person income. How in the world can someone accept such riches without thanks? Since so few people say thank you, you will stand out when you do. (See Appendix 6A for a sample thank you note for a referral.)

The most memorable thank you is a gift. An estate planning specialist in Tampa, Florida, takes a picture of his new clients and puts the picture on a plaque and sends the plaque to the referral sources. Some referral sources, he says, have a wall of plaques and actually compete with other referral sources to see who has the most plaques. Another friend of mine sends me very fine Christmas gifts every year. I would send business to that friend regardless of whether he sent me a gift, but the gift certainly makes an impression and makes the relationship special.

Events

Events can be excellent marketing tools. Examples include holiday parties, golf tournaments, deep-sea fishing excursions, seminars, and cocktail parties. One key to a successful marketing event is to carefully select the event that the people you want to influence will enjoy and remember. Do not just select an event because *you* think it would be fun. A well-run, fun event that does not influence people to send you business is not a successful marketing event. On the other hand, the event that you select as being fun to potential referral sources must also be fun to you because making your personal life and business life compatible is critical to success.

Another key element to marketing success with events is to make the event an *institution*. In other words, plan the event so that it will take place every year at the same time, thereby allowing people to enjoy the event and then enjoy looking forward to it again the next year. This not only creates top-of-mind awareness through anticipation, but also bonds you to your referral source.

The marketing success of events is enhanced by selecting something unique. For example, if most lawyers in town are already having winter holiday parties, it will be hard for you to distinguish your party and create top-of-mind awareness. The competition might also make it hard to draw a healthy crowd. To distinguish yourself, then, pick a different time to have your party.

Marketing events for former divorce clients are difficult to plan because most divorce clients desire privacy. But this does not mean they cannot be invited to events. One event I held for former clients was a "divorce client seminar." I made lists of ten to twelve of my past clients with whom I had a good relationship and invited them to my office to meet and socialize with other past clients. I held the event for two groups of women, who chose to meet over lunch. We discussed the divorce experience, what they learned, and how our firm could improve our service. The husbands of all these women had committed adultery, and the discussions in the group were very therapeutic. Listening to their discussions taught me a great deal about what it was like to go through divorce and the kind of representation I had given them. I also had a group of men. They preferred to meet on Friday afternoon at 4:00 and have some beer. Almost every one of them had committed adultery, and it was interesting to hear them discuss their regret. Of course, the beer flowed and the men had a good time.

Sponsorships

Sponsoring events is a viable way to market, though this method is very indirect, and only rarely will you receive business directly from such an effort. However, sponsoring events is a vital part of the total package of top-of-mind awareness and credibility. Sponsorships include golf hole sponsorships, charitable events such as the Kidney Foundation, Cancer League, Junior League, 100 Black

Men events, symphony and opera league, Little League, and YMCA teams. Our firm does all of these things.

I always sponsor my daughters' soccer and YMCA basketball teams. The sponsorship places the firm name on the jerseys for the team, which signals that I am giving back to the community and so creates credibility for me. What is more, I find that the kids wear the jerseys even when they are not playing and perhaps years after the season is over. So in a sense they become walking billboards.

Buy as many sponsorships in local charitable events as you can afford. Spend just enough to get a couple of tickets and program listing and charge this expense to advertising. This money is well spent since charitable events are usually attended by successful people with lots of money. In addition, contributions to local charities enhance the reputation of the firm as a credible, upright contributor to the welfare of the community as a whole.

The "Marketing Walk"

With all of the media and technology available for marketing, one of the best tools is a simple walk around town. In 1988, when I first started my business, I rented space that was not in a downtown area. I did this at a time when everyone believed that a lawyer had to be downtown to get work. To negate the fact that I was not downtown, I came up with a solution: the marketing walk. Here is hour it works. You select a location for lunch "downtown," which is likely to be frequented by lawyers or businesspeople. You arrive just enough before noon to make sure you get a seat. You make it a point to sit where you will have command of the room, so that you can catch the eye of everyone you know who comes in, and say "hello." Then, make sure you finish lunch at twenty minutes to one o'clock so that you will have time for your walk. You leave the restaurant and walk around the downtown area for fifteen minutes. Don't walk to your car; walk around. If you have picked the right area, you will see many of your potential referral sources in that fifteen-minute walk. This leads to "top-of-mind awareness" and referrals. I have always believed that I can "scare up" at least one referral in any properly executed marketing walk.

Hire a College Student

Most lawyers feel they do not have time to write letters, design a web site, write a brochure, or schedule a party, or the budget to hire a marketing director. The solution is to hire a student. Call the local college marketing department and tell them you need a student to assist you part time on your marketing. Ask for someone who is bright, energetic, and ambitious. In a few hours a week, the right student can help you accomplish great things with your marketing. The student will find the experience rewarding, and you will have excellent help at a reduced price.

Consistency

Make sure that all of your marketing attempts have a consistent image, for consistency enhances the public's awareness of your product. The more sophisticated of these business marketers zealously guard their brand and its presentation; they will not allow you, for example, to alter their trademark or name one bit. The design must be the same; the colors must be the same. You should be the same way with your marketing. For example, if you have a style or logo on your letterhead, make sure that same style of print or character is used on all items of marketing—from business cards to large envelopes, to your e-mail signature, to the jerseys of sports teams you might sponsor. (For more information on marketing, see *Marketing Your Services*[6] and *Marketing Without Advertising.*[7])

Notes

1. Sayles, Ginie, *How to Meet the Rich* (New York: Berkley Books, 1999).
2. Stanley, Thomas, and William D. Danko, *The Millionaire Next Door* (Atlanta: Longstreet Press, 1996).
3. Personal conversation with Jay Foonberg.
4. Ibid.

5. Stanley and Danko, *The Millionaire Next Door.*

6. Putman, Anthony O., *Marketing Your Services* (New York: John Wiley & Sons, 1990).

7. Phillips, Michael, and Salli Raspberry, *Marketing Without Advertising* (Berkeley, CA: Nolo Press, 1996).

Intake of the New Client

7

WHEN POTENTIAL NEW BUSINESS CALLS, you must respond promptly—within hours. People who have a family law problem are in pain, they may be terrified, and they want help NOW! Failure to return the calls of potential new customers immediately will result in the loss of a lot of business. Just this week I was trying to locate two attorneys in another state to help with an interstate custody case. It took me a week to finally hook up with one of them. I grew very frustrated during that week and was just about to call a third lawyer, when one of them finally reached me. I had originally intended to interview the two lawyers and select the one that was best, but after a week of waiting, I did not even bother to pursue lawyer number two. He finally called, but it was too late. I probably experience the same frustration every time I try to associate a lawyer on a case. This is a ridiculous situation. New client calls should be your first priority, because new clients are the life blood of your future.

Create Systems to Cover You

If you are unable to immediately return new business calls, set up a system that will cover you. Have a

57

trusted staff member be responsible for responding to new business calls when you cannot do so yourself. The staff person will call the prospective client, advise the client of your inability to call them back, and then arrange an appointment for you to return the call when your schedule allows. Alternatively, train a staff member to screen new business calls. If the client passes the screening, the staff member will have authority to set up an appointment for you with the client. Whatever system you establish, the goal should be to let no new business call go unanswered by the end of the day.

Screening

Screening, the process of making sure there is a proper fit between the law firm and the client, should take place at the time the first contact is made with the prospective client. The fit should be determined before the appointment is ever made and should continue until the contract is signed. Not all new business is good business. Do not just accept work for anybody who calls.

Careful selection of clients is critical to success. When I first started my practice, I asked a local office supply store owner what advice he had for me. Without hesitation, he said, "Mark, work only for people who will pay you."

Before you can conduct an effective screening process, you must know exactly what type of client you are after, and this requires careful thought, analysis, and business planning. You must know what your firm mission is and whom you seek to serve. You must know what your prospective clients look like, where they come from, what problems they will have, and what fees they will be able to pay. As your practice advances, become more and more selective in accepting and retaining clients. In *Inside the Magic Kingdom*, Tom Connellan writes, "It's more important to acquire the customers who count than it is to count the customers you acquire."[1]

Conflict Management

The initial screening call should make conflict management its first consideration. Family lawyers have to be careful that they do not talk to competing spouses. To prevent this from happening, many systems are available to the family lawyer.

First, keep a record of every new business inquiry. Every new business call should be documented in writing. Our firm has created a new client screening checklist that is filled out with each call from a prospective client. This screening sheet is kept in a paper file and is saved in a Word Perfect file labeled "New Client Telephone Screening" (see Appendix 7A). Second, place the name of the person in a separate file in a case management system. This permits automated conflict check.

If a person comes to the office for advice, you should create a file even if the advice is only for one hour and you do not expect the client to return. If you use a case management system, the client should be placed in that system as a "client." The file may be immediately closed, but it must be set up to ensure that a conflict check will turn up the file.

I myself have at times been sloppier with conflict management than I should be, mainly because I have been a small practitioner and have always thought I could remember everyone with whom I have ever spoken. Over time, however, this can catch up to you. Last year, for example, I spent an hour with a local businessman and advised him on his divorce, which had become protracted in the hands of another lawyer. A couple of weeks later, I received a call from his wife, who had learned of my talk with her husband. She complained that I had given her an hour of advice some two years earlier. Not believing that was possible, I checked my systems, but failed to find her either in my paper file system or in my case management system. But then I remembered her: I had indeed seen her for an hour, but I had not set up a file because she said she did not want to go forward with a divorce. Fortunately, she was only concerned that I not represent her husband; I apologized and I assured her that I was ethically prevented from doing so and so would not represent him. She said thank you and was satisfied with the knowledge I could not represent either of them. I was lucky with this mistake. So, keep track of who calls and check your conflicts before you give advice.

Getting the Check

You should get the check for your fee or retainer for your time during the initial interview; the only exception is where your Code of Professional Responsibility requires otherwise. During the screening interview, it is important to let the caller know that payment is due at the initial interview. Then, at the initial interview, you should tell the client what the retainer is and ask for it. If the client is simply paying for an hour of time, ask for the check before he or she leaves. You can handle this by saying something like, "Would you like to pay by check, cash, or credit card?"

Many lawyers have told me they do not charge for the initial interview, but I would discourage this practice. I believe I can give a lifetime of advice in the first twenty minutes of interview with a client, so why should this valuable advice be given for free? Moreover, by spending time with a client and giving advice, the lawyer is forbidden from representing the other spouse. Many people have been known to visit many lawyers in an area in an attempt to prevent their spouse from using them. This is called "poisoning the well." If someone is going to "poison the well" in this fashion, he should not be permitted to do it for free.

Get the Contract Signed at the Initial Interview

In states where it is permitted, ask clients to sign the attorney–client contract at the initial interview. Tell them that the contract gives you the authority to represent them. Do not give them the contract and let them take it home and think about it. Some State Codes of Professional Responsibility require lawyers to give the clients an opinion letter and a *cooling off period* before signing the contract. If this is so in your state, follow your Code of Conduct; otherwise, establish the relationship at the initial interview. This is good, solid business practice, and, it also gives both attorney and client a clear understanding of the beginning of the representation.

Clearly establishing the beginning of representation is extremely important as a measure of protection from malpractice.

If a client comes in to see you for advice and then does not sign a contract, who is responsible for the client's representation in the ensuing days? The client will regard *you* as responsible if something goes wrong and will claim you gave them advice after which something wrong happened. They will say this even though the facts changed after the advice. If a client does not retain you, send a letter clearly stating that your representation did not continue after the initial interview and that you are not responsible for advice that changes upon changes in facts. (A copy of a form is presented in Appendix 7B.)

The Initial Interview

The initial interview has four purposes:

1. To obtain enough general information about the case to chart a basic course of action.
2. To give the client advice on how to protect him- or herself immediately.
3. To establish the relationship and contract for legal services.
4. To give the client comfort.

A variety of opinion has been expressed on how long the initial interview should last and how much detail is developed. You will have to develop your own method in this area. I recommend that you limit the initial interview to an hour or so because it is hard to assimilate much more than an hour's worth of information at one time. Conferences that last longer than an hour are usually nothing more than nonproductive chat sessions. Finally, the client may elect not to hire you, and you will not want to take the chance of not being paid for more than an hour. This happened to me just the other day. I deviated from my normal process and spent about three hours with a dysfunctional family, trying to help them sort out a problem. When they left, they told me they would send me a check, but they later refused, saying they did not like my advice and that all I had done was sit there and listen to them for three hours, running up my fee.

One risk in limiting the initial interview is that you can miss an important detail. This risk diminishes with experience. So in the earlier years of your career, you might want to err on the side of a longer conference, but do not take too long.

Create a Form or Checklist

Most experienced lawyers have checklists or standard questionnaires to eliminate the possibility of missing important information. The length and detail of these checklists vary, but all should contain the following key items.

1. Client contact and billing information
2. Basic information necessary to prepare pleadings (date of marriage and separation, names of children, past residences, etc.)
3. Financial information
4. Information supporting claims to relief, such as grounds for divorce

The questionnaire can be completed in the initial interview or be given to the client as "homework." We keep our initial questionnaire fairly simple and complete it with the client during the initial interview, thereby ensuring that we have the information at all times when we need it, instead of having to track it down from the client later. (See Appendix 7C for a New Client Questionnaire.)

One good technique to avoid misunderstandings and malpractice exposure is to have the client fill the questionnaire out herself and state what her mission or objective is with the representation. This will protect the lawyer from relying on information—or a lack of an important detail—which the client later claims is different from what the lawyer thought.

Another method of establishing the client's mission is to include it in the contract or retainer letter. Of course, the client's mission may be unreasonable. That is where the retainer letter is of value, since the lawyer may state what the mission is but qualify what is possible to obtain in court.

Warnings

Warnings must be incorporated into your initial communications with the client. For example, once a client's relationship with a spouse gets to the point that one or both of them are consulting with an attorney, clear and present danger of several kinds arises. One danger is that the other spouse will do something to the finances, such as drain a savings account or run up credit card charges. The client must be warned of such dangers and be told how to prevent them at the earliest opportunity. For example, several years ago I was about halfway through my initial interview with a woman who was telling me what a tough customer her husband was. She then disclosed their finances and the fact that they had about $100,000 in certificates of deposit at a bank in a town 90 miles north. She also disclosed that the CDs had just matured. Upon learning this, I said, "Stop right there. Leave me now and drive to the bank right now and get those certificates." She later reported that as she was driving back from the bank with the money, she passed her husband on the Interstate driving toward the bank. The best way to make sure that all of the proper warnings are given is to include them in the initial client questionnaire.

Mind, Body, Spirit

Any lawyer experienced in litigation, and with family law in particular, knows that managing the emotions of the matter is probably more important than anything else. A client who is healthy, attentive, confident, and prepared stands a much greater chance of helping his or her lawyer achieve maximum results. Clients who are emotional, angry, and resentful, or overly fearful, obstruct and interfere with the delivery of legal service. That is why it is important for the lawyer to start to work out these things with the client at the outset.

In our initial interview, we tell our clients that we want them to approach their crises from the standpoint of taking care of their minds, their bodies, and their spirit, and we tell them that the best way to take care of their minds is to get educated. We provide them with our "Divorce Client Notebook" as well as with brochures, magazines, and books dealing with their situation. For example, a woman who is complaining of abuse but is unable to articulate the abuse is given a book, such as *The Verbally Abusive Relationship*. Another example is a woman who said she wanted to try and negotiate her divorce with her husband. She was given Herb Cohen's book on negotiation, *You Can Negotiate Anything*.[2] When people educate themselves, they may not learn all they need to know, but they gain confidence from knowing that they are helping themselves; they have less fear; and they become better at discussing their case and digesting the meaning of events.

In terms of their bodies, we suggest that clients monitor their diet carefully, eating healthy foods such as fruits and vegetables. A healthy diet enhances performance and elevates mood, both of which are necessary tools for enduring crises. We also suggest that they exercise regularly. For those who have not exercised before coming to you, it can be suggested that they develop a morning ritual of getting up at sunrise and walking for a half hour. Exercise produces many positive effects, such as preparing the body for the difficulties of the day, enhancing mood, and reducing the effects of stress.

Finally, clients should take care of their spirits. The spirit is the most important part of the human makeup. Without a healthy spirit, everything else breaks down. We therefore require all of our clients to receive regular, scheduled therapy with a mental health counselor. I explain that I require therapy not because I think they are mentally disturbed but because they are going through perhaps the worst experience of their lives and so should have a well-trained person guide them through it. As an example, I describe Mammoth Cave, a huge cave in Kentucky that is beautiful, with unimaginable and wondrous sites. But it is also a dangerous labyrinth, which, if entered without a guide, could prove deadly. A counselor, then, serves as a guide to help you get through your crisis safely, and perhaps even see some beauty along the way. Most people understand advice couched in these terms.

Your clients can take care of their spirit through conducting meditation, taking personal time, going on sabbatical, or worshiping at religious services on a regular basis. You should explain that you deal with crises every day and that to deal with crises effectively, you must pay careful attention not only to your mind and body, but also your spirit. After all, taking good care of your mind, body, and spirit is not a bad thing and carries no downside.

The mind–body–spirit approach both helps the client and sends positive service signals. The client knows he is getting caring counsel and that he is receiving a service that exceeds what he expected.

Taking Clients from Other Lawyers

Often you will receive calls from people who are represented by other lawyers and are unhappy and want to make a change. You should be wary of a difficult client who has hired several different lawyers; in particular you should be careful that you are not simply setting yourself up with a difficult client. When you get a call from such clients, you should ask the following basic questions:

1. Who was their prior lawyer?
2. What is the problem?
3. Have they attempted to resolve the problem?
4. Have they paid their prior lawyer?

You want to know who the lawyer is because that usually gives you a perspective on whether the problem lies with the lawyer or with the client. You want to know what the problem is for the same reason. You want to know if they have attempted to resolve the problem because that is something they should do before making a change. It is possible that a misunderstanding can be resolved and that the representation can continue; it is usually not in their best interests to make a change if they do not have to. Divorce litigation is difficult and emotional, and making an unnecessary change could send a signal of "division in the ranks" to the other side. I also do not want to take on a new client who does not have the honesty and courtesy to attempt to resolve problems before moving on.

As for paying the prior attorney's bill before undertaking representation of a dissatisfied client, I believe that all lawyers should refuse to take on a new client until they have satisfactorily resolved billing issues with the prior lawyer. This protects the prior lawyer as much as it does you: If they cheat him out of his bill, they will likely do it to you.

Taking over representation from a prior lawyer is dangerous at best, because you are stepping into someone else's mess. The transfer of representation must be handled quickly but carefully. Our firm has developed a checklist for this, which is presented in Appendix 7D.

Do not take your new client's word for the status of matters or accept your client's supply of pleadings as accurate. The second you begin representation, call the court clerk to determine exactly what is on the docket and make sure no hearing is set for the next day. Then you should immediately obtain the court file to verify the status of the pleadings, to make sure that requests for admissions, for example, were not due yesterday. Call opposing counsel to find out as much as you can.

Maintaining Good Clients

After you have elected to represent someone, you should continually evaluate whether the client is, in fact, someone who is well suited to your firm. Create an "ABCD" list of criteria for clients and constantly analyze your clients in relation to this list. The A client is the perfect client, the D client is the client from hell, and so on. In order to have a healthy business, you should constantly be "culling" your client base of C and D clients. (Our firm's ABCD list is presented in Appendix 7E.) You should develop your own list.

Notes

1. Connellan, Tom, *Inside the Magic Kingdom*, p. 158 (Austin, TX: Bard Press, 1997).

2. Evans, Patricia, *The Verbally Abusive Relationship* (Holbrook, MA: Adams Media Corporation, 1996); Cohen, Herb, *You Can Negotiate Anything* (Secaucus, NJ: L. Stuart, 1980).

Fees and Billing 8

THE FIRST MISTAKE MOST LAWYERS MAKE in collecting fees is to fail to address the issue of costs honestly at the beginning of the relationship. Surveys show that the last thing attorneys want to talk about is fees but surveys of clients prove that clients do want to hear about them. Even clients who are not fee shopping want to know what things will cost. In the initial contact with the firm, then, potential clients should be advised of hourly rates and initial retainers and should be told if there is a fee for the initial interview.

Many lawyers do not know how to broach the subject of fees. In the initial screening call with the potential client, ask basic questions designed to quickly determine if the person is calling with a divorce matter, if a conflict exists, and if the firm serves this type of client. Neither client nor attorney is well served if a businesslike approach is not taken to quickly determine if the two are right for each other. After learning the necessary information, simply say, "Let me tell you how we charge. Our firm requires a $5,000 retainer. Our attorneys charge varying rates, depending on expertise and experience, from $250 per hour to $150 per hour. Our paralegal rate is $80." These phrases convey several things to the client. The "let me tell you how we charge"

67

exhibits ease and confidence in dealing with fees. It also conveys the notion that there is an *institution* and not just some lone lawyer asking for money. Notice the use of the word "requires." That word conveys the notion that the matter is not up for negotiation. It also conveys all of the necessary information in very clear, concise terms.

Setting Fees

In setting fees, consult your state's code of professional responsibility, which should show standards for setting fees. Next, find out what other lawyers in your area are charging. Consult with close lawyer and judge friends to see what they know others are charging. Call lawyers with varying levels of experience and say something like: "I am calling you because you are at the top of your trade, and I need your help in setting fees that are appropriate for a person of my experience. Would you mind telling me what you know about what lawyers are charging in our area?"

Once you find out what others are charging, analyze what rate will fulfill your business mission. For example, in the early years of your practice, you might charge a moderate rate. This is appropriate for your level of experience. If you were to charge a high rate, you might lose possible business because your experience does not command a high rate. On the other hand, you do not want to charge a low rate, because you want your services to be taken seriously. After you gain a foothold, you may decide to charge a rate that is just below the higher rates. The purpose is to attempt to get a toehold in the higher levels of business by billing yourself as just as competent as the top lawyers, but not as expensive. Then, later, as you take your place among the most experienced of divorce lawyers, you should charge as much as they do.

Types of Fees

Flat Fee

Prior to the 1970s, the most common method of charging was probably the flat fee. Then the U.S. Supreme Court decided that fee schedules were unconstitutional. Since that decision, and with the growing influence of insurance companies, the flat fee has faded in prominence. Although flat fees are in use in some areas, flat fees are tough to use in cases that are not simple. There is no way to know, at the beginning, what the course of litigation will be. A case that appears to be all about finances can suddenly become an intense custody battle. Once the fee is set, it is very difficult, if not impossible, to change. Flat fees can encourage abuse by either the attorney or the client. A client may engage in excessive litigation and take tough positions, believing that the expense for it will lie on his attorney's shoulders, the fee having been already set. The attorney may sell a client short or fail to take appropriate measures, feeling that he will not receive any more money for the effort.

If an attorney really knows his market and what it takes to get a case solved, flat fees may be a key to success. I have seen this primarily in rural areas where there are judges who take tight control of cases. They set many cases on the docket during short terms of court. Rural attorneys appear in court during the short terms with many cases on the docket. The judge handles many cases in chambers and is able to mediate settlement of the cases. This allows the lawyer to believe with some confidence that his cases are not likely to get out of hand, and to charge, therefore, a reasonable flat fee. Clients like the flat fee because they know what their case is going to cost.

For additional resources on flat fee billing, see:

Calloway, James A., and Mark A. Robertson, eds. *Winning Alternatives to the Billable Hour: Strategies That Work.* 2d ed. Chicago: American Bar Association, 2002.

Baker, Ronald J. *Professional's Guide to Value Pricing.* 5th ed. New York: Aspen Publishers, 2004.

Reed, Richard C., ed. *Beyond the Billable Hour: An Anthology of Alternative Billing Methods.* Chicago: American Bar Association, 1989.

Reed, Richard C., ed. *Win-Win Billing Strategies: Alternatives That Satisfy Your Clients and You.* Chicago: American Bar Association, 1992.

Hourly Fee

The most common form of billing in the divorce world is the hourly fee. Attorneys record their time in predetermined intervals and charge the client according to the time spent. The most common intervals are either quarter hour intervals or sixth of hour intervals. For example, under the quarter hour interval method, the minimum charge for any effort is at least fifteen minutes. Under the sixth of hour method, the minimum charge for any activity is ten minutes.

Value Billing

Many Codes of Professional Responsibility allow for so-called value billing. What this means is that you may charge a greater amount for something that does not take much time, where there is great value in the task. For example, if you have devised a very lengthy, informative letter that explains certain aspects of a case to clients, you may consider billing more than the few minutes it takes you to generate the letter after its initial preparation. Or you may have learned how to mechanize preparation of discovery or pleadings and thereby charge more than the few minutes it takes you to prepare the pleading after its original development. Check your local code of professional conduct regarding value billing before using it.

Contingency

Contingency charging involves taking a percentage of the amount collected on behalf of the client. State Codes of Professional Responsibility generally do not permit his method of charging except in child support arrearage cases where contingency fees are generally permitted.

Retainers

To operate a successful family law practice, the lawyer must use retainers: a certain amount of money that is obtained in advance of the work. This retainer is placed in a trust account and used as a reserve for the attorney to charge against. Abraham Lincoln, a great trial lawyer, believed that a retainer was important because the lawyer then knew he had a client and the client knew he had a lawyer.

The amount of the retainer should be determined on the basis of factors much the same as those used to set an hourly rate or a flat fee. First, review what other lawyers are charging in your area. Next, analyze what type of retainer would most further your firm mission. If you are just beginning to develop your practice, you may want to quote low retainers in order to garner more business. In the latter stages, your retainer will go up, depending on your experience, expertise, and place among other lawyers in your community.

Retainers can be either refundable or nonrefundable. In a refundable retainer, the amount of retainer left in trust after charges is refunded to the client upon closure of the case or termination of the representation. In a nonrefundable retainer, the retainer is not refunded. The attorney simply keeps whatever is left, whether or not the work has been billed.

A nonrefundable retainer can create extra income for a lawyer if the lawyer is able to conclude the work before the expenditure of the retainer through time billings. This may benefit clients in that the attorney will have the incentive to act aggressively to bring the case to a quick solution. It could also work against a client's interests in causing the attorney to do less than what might be necessary to do an appropriate amount of work on the case or to settle the case properly. Check the rules in your jurisdiction before utilizing a nonrefundable retainer.

"Poisoning the Well"

The nonrefundable retainer discourages "lawyer shopping" or "poisoning the well." As noted earlier, when a lawyer establishes a reputation in divorce law, it is not uncommon for prospective divorce clients to visit several top lawyers in an attempt to conflict them out of the case. They then use another lawyer for the work. The nonrefundable retainer will either discourage this conduct or at least make the perpetrator pay a handsome price for this unscrupulous behavior.

End Retainer

The end retainer is a method of holding a certain portion of the retainer until the end. The lawyer receives the retainer at the beginning of the representation but does not use it. Instead, the client is expected to pay the bill as it is incurred, so the retainer is not used. Then, when the work is concluded, the attorney has the certainty of knowing a retainer is there to pay that much of the final bill. Some experts in law practice management believe this is an effective collection tool because the client has the least incentive to pay the bill at the conclusion of the work or when the result is not what the client wanted.

How to Bill

Carefully Plan Your Day

Careful planning greatly enhances performance. Do not start a workday without taking at least fifteen minutes to plan what you will work on. Advanced planning also involves planning *when* you will work on something. You should create a simple list of what you are going to do, prioritize the list and set up at least three categories, based on three questions: "What *must* I accomplish today?"; "What would I *like* to accomplish today?"; and "What do I not want to *forget* to work on this week?" In planning your day, start to work on the projects that *must* be completed that day. Learning to prioritize will prevent the inefficiency and unpleasantness of simply responding to emergencies all day long.

Another important matter to consider in planning your day is to make sure that the activities on your "to do" list will generate income. If something does not generate income, it should not be listed as an item that *must* be completed that day. You must pay the bills first before you do anything, or you will not be in business long.

Record Time Contemporaneously

Some lawyers do not keep track of their time, so that on the day they decide to bill, they will go back through the file, look at what they have done, and attempt to reconstruct a bill. This method is inaccurate and may lead to overcharging the client. The more likely scenario though is that it will lead to extreme *under*charging. Studies have shown that lawyers lose large amounts of time if they do not record their time simultaneous to doing the work. Even if you wait a couple of hours before recording time, you will not remember what you have done.

If you use a time sheet method, where you manually record the time, keep the time sheet on your desk on the side of the desk where you rest your writing hand. Record the activity as you do it. For example, if you are about to make a phone call, pick up your pen, write the call on your time sheet, and record the time at the end of the call.

Check Yourself Periodically

At different intervals during the day, check your time. If it is noon and you only have one hour of time on your sheet, go back in your mind through the morning and see if you can remember some activity that you did not write down. If you do not recall some missed time, keep in mind that you are behind on the day and that you need to pick up the pace of your billing activity the rest of the day. Activities, such as short calls and letters, will help you pick up lost time.

Case Management Systems

Case management software is a great innovation that has improved billing, helping you to automatically bill for many activities and to record your time with less time and effort than if you were doing it manually.

Any lawyer knows that it is very hard to bill for an entire day. If you do not know what you are doing, you can work all day but end up with only half a day of billings. To make life easier, you should avail yourself of every technique there is to recoup the true value of your efforts.

Make a Call, Write a Letter

Each task can command a minimum time entry. For example, an eight-minute call merits a quarter hour time entry. A letter that took only ten minutes to create would likewise be worthy of a quarter hour time entry. If these two activities are billed, the total time entry will be one half hour, or thirty minutes, but the actual time spent will be only eighteen minutes. Therefore, in order to help you obtain billing that more closely reflects your effort, these activities should be grouped together whenever possible. For example, if you are negotiating a matter with an opposing counsel, the activity will require one call to the opposing counsel and another to the client to discuss the call with the opposing counsel. Each call should be documented with a letter. So, you make a call to the opposing counsel and document the discussion with a letter. Then you discuss the call with the client and document the client's instructions in a letter to the client. The whole activity might take twenty-three minutes, but it will justify a billing entry of one hour. The calls and documentation of the calls not only enhance performance and service to the client, but also prevent malpractice situations.

Task Clustering

The task clustering technique combines similar activities in one block of time, leading to higher efficiency and higher billing. For example, make a list of all the phone calls you need to make and block out an hour to make all of the calls in rapid succession. You might be able to make seven calls in the hour. Each call will merit a quarter hour time entry. Thus, you will have spent one hour but will bill for one hour and forty-five minutes. If you combine the task clustering technique with the make a call, write a letter technique, you may be able to double the billing. These techniques are absolutely necessary to recover time, which is almost always mysteriously lost during the day.

Time Blocking

Time blocking is a time management technique that can be used to capture the lawyer's true effort. It calls for "blocking" time on the calendar to perform certain activities in a case. Used to its optimum, the technique can help you plan an entire week of work and billing in advance by blocking the time to do the activities in each file. For example, you might block out 1:00 to 3:00 to work on discovery in the Jones case and 3:00 to 5:00 to work on a motion in the Smith case. The blocking of the time will focus your efforts and result in a solid billing of the entire time set aside. It will also help prevent distractions from the task, which can dilute billing. Staff should be enlisted in the time blocking to prevent phone calls from being put through, as well as other distractions.

Time blocking should be used to plan the performance of tasks well in advance. This will decrease "panic-driven" work. For example, examine what cases you have set for trial in the future. Then carefully decide when you will need to accomplish certain tasks. If you need to have research completed prior to trial for a "trial brief," block out time on your calendar about ten days before the trial to research and write the brief. Actually, you can create an appointment for yourself to perform work such as witness interviews and client preparation conferences between certain hours. Once you have mastered this technique, you will find that you are not staying up all night the day before a trial scrambling to get everything done. Such planning enhances billing and creates more efficient use of your energy—which also enhances billing in the long term.

Forms and Letters—Value Billing

Every opportunity to multiply effort should be used to capture value. Value is multiplied by the use of forms. There is no reason to perform any task twice. Over time, you will find that you have already done what you are about to do. There is no reason to reinvent the wheel. Every attempt should be made to preserve effort in a form and to store the form in a place where it can easily be found and used.

If you do not have software, create a form notebook. Structure your forms in a generic fashion so that they can be used for as many different cases and situations as possible. The best use of forms derives from document assembly software and allows you to "merge" specific client information into the form. The document is customized in an automated fashion. This method is enhanced if highly trained support staff gain the experience to create the document for you. This leads to a legitimate billing for the attorney, with only a small amount of review time expended.

Arrive at the Office Early

One of the best techniques for increasing your effectiveness is to arrive at the office as early as 7:30 A.M., using your first fifteen minutes after you arrive to carefully plan your day. You should then go right to work and not permit distractions. Thus you should be able to place two solid hours of billable time on your time sheet by 10:00 A.M. This head start on the day creates confidence, enthusiasm, and momentum. In contrast, if you arrive at work at 9:00 A.M., you may not get started billing until 9:30, so that you are immediately behind and feel you have to scramble. Others will be in the office and will likely create distractions that may prevent you from starting your work. Phone calls will be coming in, and you will get sidetracked from planning your time, thereby making you lose control of the day and your time. You will find yourself staying at the office well after 6:00 P.M., so that you can catch up on your hours. You will get home late and very tired, feeling deprived of family and relaxation time.

Bill Collection

Timely, Regular Billing

One key to efficient collection is to send bills at the same time every month, notably the first of the month. This creates a rhythm and expectation for the client. Most people sit down and pay their bills on a certain day each month. The mortgage, the electricity, the car note, the cable bill, are all sent on the first of the month; send yours then too.

Great pains should be taken to send bills at the same time. If you have associates or partners, encourage them to cooperate in recording their time for billing by the end of the month. You simply cannot afford to have a partner, associate, employee, or bookkeeper who does not regard the matter of timely mailing of bills as a matter of life and death for your business.

Billing upon Completion of the Task

One time when it is okay to deviate from regular billing is upon completion of the task. For example, if you have just completed a trial that has ended in a favorable result, attempt to send the bill to the client immediately. This way, the bill will arrive in close proximity to the client's witnessing of your effort and their euphoria over a good result. This will increase the client's willingness to pay you: he or she may even be *glad* to send you a check. In contrast, if you wait to bill clients for weeks or months after you have completed their project, their willingness to pay the bill will decrease dramatically with every passing day, *even if you obtained an incredible result for them.*

Talking to the Client

It is important to talk to your clients about fees, both candidly and often. Tell them the cost of the things they ask for in an unemotional, professional way. My favorite example of this approach comes from the movie *Kramer vs. Kramer.* Dustin Hoffman has just lost custody of his child to Meryl Streep, and he is talking with his lawyer about what to do. The lawyer has a glass of scotch, and when Dustin Hoffman emotionally protests the trial result, the lawyer calmly replies, "You can appeal, but it will cost you $20,000." Hoffman elects not to appeal. It is very important for lawyers to model this scene. The communication about the cost of the course of action was unemotional and informative, and the client was left with a clear picture of what lay ahead. The client was given the information necessary to formulate his decision, and, if he had elected to appeal, he and the lawyer would know and understand that $20,000 was necessary to start the work.

If clients do not pay their fees, or are late in paying them, communication must be immediate. If a client does not pay the bill in ten days, then you know there may be trouble. If a client does not pay in thirty days, then he or she does not intend to pay at all. Therefore, good billing practices call for communication with the clients at the ten- and thirty-day marks. This communication must never be emotional or angry; rather, it should always be positive and should assume that the client intends to pay. For example, you should never call a client and say, "You haven't paid me in thirty days, and I am going to stop work if you don't pay me immediately." Such a statement will alienate the client and make it difficult to continue the relationship. The client who feels the relationship may not continue is even less likely to send you his or her hard-earned dollars. Instead, the ten-day call might go something like this: "I was just calling to make sure that you were satisfied with the statement we mailed you on the first of the month and wondering if you have placed a check in the mail." A thirty-day call might go like this: "Our statement for services rendered to you is now thirty days late. I was wondering if there is a problem with our service which we need to address. Is there any problem with you addressing our fees at this time?" At times clients will complain about the bill and say it is too much. The response to that complaint is to say that you want to address their concerns about the bill and ask them if they have a copy of it with them. Then, ask them what billing entry they find objectionable. It is important not to get caught in the trap of discussing in general terms whether the bill is "too high"; instead, go over specific time entries. This technique usually shows the client has no complaint. However, it may show you a mistake or an overcharge. Finally, if a client complains about some time entries, say: "I have reviewed these entries and I find them to be legitimate and necessary, but I value our relationship and would like to do something for you. What if I cut the time for the deposition preparation in half? Would that make you happy?" (Some people say you should never cut a bill because it makes the client suspicious that you overcharged them in the first place. You will have to determine for yourself whether or not it is best to make customer service reductions.)

Another technique for getting paid is to bargain for a smaller amount in exchange for immediate payment. For example, a client is complaining that a $7,500 bill is too much. You need the money to make your payroll on the fifteenth, so you do not want to wait for the client to pay the bill in installments. So, you say something like this: "I know the bill is a lot, but I know it was necessary to get the result we achieved. You have been a great client. I want to do something for you on the bill, but I need something for me in exchange. What if I reduced the bill to $5,000 in exchange for you bringing a check to me tomorrow? Would that be good for you?" Most clients jump at the chance to get the discount.

Never Get Angry

Whatever you do, never lose your temper with a client. Do not snap at the client and do not issue a threat for not paying your bill. First, few, if any, people respond well to negative communication. Second, as a lawyer you occupy a high position and should not unnecessarily expose yourself to the risk of disciplinary action. Clients who have been yelled at, intimidated, threatened, or insulted will look for any available means to get back at you, from telling everybody they can to filing a bar complaint. Therefore, always, at all costs, stay positive in your communications. Even if this approach does not appear to work in the short run, it may work in the long run, or at least, it will make bar complaints less likely.

Letter of Thanks for Payment

Too often, human beings spend all of their time addressing improper conduct and not enough time reinforcing positive conduct. Therefore, any collections program should include positive reinforcement for timely payment of the bill. The easiest and least costly measure to reinforce positive conduct is to commend and thank the person. When you receive a nice check from someone, send a thank you card and write something like: "Thank you for your recent payment of our bill. You always pay your bills in a timely fashion, and I cannot tell you how much I appreciate it. I know paying legal bills is hard, and it shows a lot about your character that you work so hard to take care of us. Thank you!"

Another way to encourage timely payment of the bill is to offer a discount. Our firm routinely offers a 5 percent discount for payment by the tenth of the month. Many clients take advantage of this and appreciate our call on the tenth to remind them they can take advantage of this discount if they will get their check in that day.

Personal Notes on the Bill

At billing time, sit down with your bills and make personal notes on each bill. Clients appreciate the personal, handwritten notes on their bills. It makes them feel that you have reviewed the bill and have personally made sure it was right and that it was not just generated by some impersonal computer. Here are some examples of such notes:

"Bobby, just want you to know that our firm cares about you."

"Susie, we love working for you."

"Jim, thanks for providing the resources for us to do a good job for you."

"Mike, I am pleased with the way things are going and hope you are too."

"It's been a long road, but it looks like we are about through."

"Baby needs milk, send money."

Fee Agreement

Always obtain a written fee agreement. Such agreements may or not be required in your state by the Code of Professional Responsibility, but they are critical to fee collection and to avoiding complaint from the bar. (Appendix 8A contains an hourly billing contract, and Appendices 8B and 8C contain fixed fee contracts.)

Fee Questions

Lawyers are typically defensive when presented with questions about fees; this is a mistake. Clients should be encouraged to ask about fees. Tell clients something like, "Look, the hourly billing method is simply a method of charging. It is not carved in stone. If you ever have a question about a charge, I will be more than happy to discuss it with you and review the charge."

Over the years, I have had many clients come to me from other lawyers and complain that they called to question their lawyer about their bill and the lawyer reacted angrily. This defensiveness leads clients to believe the lawyer has something to hide and so ends up in problems. Another response of many lawyers is to ignore the complaint and hope it goes away. This creates long-term, deep-seated resentment on the part of the client. The first inkling of complaint about fees should be met with an immediate, nondefensive call to the client to address his or her concern. The lawyer should say, "I understand you have a question about our charges, and I wanted to get together with you as soon as possible to address your concerns and assuage your fears." Then, ask the client for *specific* complaints about specific time entries.

Tracking the Retainer

Most lawyers get some kind of retainer, and that is good. But most lawyers probably continue to work on cases with no concept of whether they are being paid, or whether the retainer is exhausted, or whether they ever will get paid. This is bad for the client, and it is certainly bad for the lawyer. It is bad for the client for many reasons. First, the lawyer may be running up charges a client cannot pay, which no well-meaning client appreciates. Second, running up bills that clients do not pay creates a debtor–creditor relationship that creates significant stress in the more important relationship: the attorney–client relationship. Along these lines, I find that it is human nature for us to resent the people we owe. You, as the lawyer, may feel that you are doing something honorable by continuing to work without being paid and building up a debt. The truth of the matter is that such clients do not appreciate you at all; they resent you because they owe you money!!

To prevent client debt, track the status of the retainer carefully and in a timely manner. There are several ways to do this.

The first is to utilize an automated billing system that will allow you to review the status of trust accounts at the intervals you select, such as weekly or monthly. Another way is to utilize a case docket, which includes account and trust account information.

Educating the Client

An essential element of successful collections is early client education. The client must be told at the outset of the relationship what the fees are, the unpredictability of the final bill, and the things that make the bill increase. There should be no mincing of words about fees. When clients ask, "What will a divorce cost?" respond by saying, "There is no way to predict the cost; it depends entirely on how much disagreement there is." If people want to go further with this, then say something like the following: "We have done a survey of our cases, and we find they fall into three basic categories. The first is the category where the parties are able to agree on things fairly quickly. This happens in 25 percent of our cases and the range of cost is anywhere from $750 to $7,500. The second range includes 50 percent of our cases, and this cost ranges from $10,000 to $15,000. The third range is the difficult litigation range, and that is from $40,000 to $100,00." If you keep accurate data on your cases, you will be able to give the clients the accurate figures. This helps you to advise clients on the front end as to what to expect. I find that people will accept just about anything if they have received advance warning. That is why early education on the amount of fees makes bill collection easier.

Initial Interview

Early education of the client begins in the client screening and in the initial interview. Our firm has an initial interview checklist, which you may find at the conclusion of our Standard Client Intake Form in Appendix 7A. This checklist requires us to tell the client in the initial interview certain things about fees: first, the retainer is not a flat fee or an estimate of the cost. I cannot tell you how many people have tried to tell me or the bookkeeper that I said that cost was going to be a certain amount. When they say that, I counter, "Well, Mrs. Jones, I not only didn't say that, I wouldn't ever have said that because the cost is totally unpredictable and I have a note here on my initial interview notes where I told you—as I tell all of my clients—that the cost is totally unpredictable."

Client Information

One way to make clients feel good about fees is to give them "product." It is very hard for lawyers to deliver "product" because the true value of what we do lies in *thinking*. Therefore, we must be creative in delivering tangible product to the client. Copies of work product and informational materials are key to giving the client something tangible.

At the initial interview, provide clients with a wealth of informational materials such as the Divorce Client Notebook, magazines such as the ABA *Family Advocate*, legal standards in your state for divorce, equitable distribution, alimony, custody, and support. (You can access our "Divorce Client Notebook" in the FAQ section of our web page at Chinnandassociates.com.) In addition, explain cost-saving measures such as mediation and provide the client with brochures on the mediation process. Finally, give the clients books on abuse, relationships, or negotiation.

Civility 9

Our job as lawyers is to resolve civil disputes *civilly*. Law is designed to replace the resolution of disputes through force or violence. Isn't it logical then that civility and courtesy should be the commitment of every lawyer?

Several years ago a young man hired me right after discovering that his wife was having an affair. He was extremely distraught. He had been married for a long time and had two young children. I counseled him to remain calm and "let the dust settle." I soon learned that the woman had gone to see a lawyer whom I considered to be a friend. I told my client, "Relax, I have this under control, the opposing counsel is a friend of mine." That was on a Friday. On Monday morning at 8:00 A.M., my lawyer "friend" had the sheriff serve my client with a lawsuit at his work, without warning. My client flew into a rage. He cried at me, "I thought you said you had this under control!" My friend's tactic made me angry and I retaliated. The case deteriorated, and my friend and I fought a nasty custody and adultery battle. Things got nastier and nastier until all the parties and lawyers were forever alienated.

You can avoid this horrible outcome by sticking to the following civility rules:

1. *Never retaliate.* Whenever a lawyer does something mean or sends a nasty letter, the great temptation is to retaliate. You should never do so. Simply ignore nasty letters. And if you must respond, which is rare, craft the letter carefully to make sure there is no hint of concern about the nasty words in the initiating letter. If a lawyer sets a hearing at the last minute without giving you notice, do not respond with anger; act like nothing bothers you. Herb Cohen, in *Negotiate This!*, writes, "Even in the face of provocations, don't get ruffled or riled but remain placid and untroubled."[1]

One way to look at this in sports terms is that you do not want the other team to dictate the way the game will be played. You must stick to your game plan. If their game is cheap shots and throwing elbows, you will ignore it and continue to play the game the way *you* think it should be played. If you start throwing elbows, you will forget how you play the game and you will lose.

2. *Never, never send a nasty letter.* Before you send a nasty letter to another lawyer, think about whether you have ever been impressed favorably when *you have received one.* The answer, "Never." In fact, the nasty letter not only does not change someone's mind, but it usually makes the receiver more determined to prove the sender wrong. It operates more like a red flag in front of a bull than a conduct changer. Despite this obvious truth, lawyers are known as masters of the nasty letter.

In one recent case, I had cordial conversations with the opposing counsel, but nonetheless received horrible letters from him. I never responded to his letters in writing. Instead, every time I received such a letter, I picked up the phone and had a nice sociable chat with him. Along the way, I would say something like "I got your letter. You seemed quite upset with me. What did I do?" This approach seemed to disarm him. Soon, my positive personal response to his letters had a positive effect on him. This lawyer, notorious as a tough old codger, is now one of my biggest fans— and I am one of his. This positive change took place because I never took the bait, but instead showed him respect in calling him and talking to him.

If you must send a nasty letter—which should happen extremely rarely—give the other attorney a warning call, such as, "Well Jim, your client has not been able to leave my client alone, despite my requests, so I am afraid I am going to have to send you a nasty letter. I hate to do it, but I feel like I must in order to protect my client. Do you think you could speak to your client and put an end to this?" This type of call allows you to make your point, without alienating the other counsel. It is also more likely to produce the desired conduct.

3. *Talk to opposing counsel.* When you find that another lawyer is involved in a case, or when you enter an appearance in a case, call the opposing counsel. You do this to establish rapport and civility. Do not take any action or file any pleading without calling the opposing counsel to state what you are about to do and why, and perhaps to work it out before you do act on it. Of course, there are the rare times when it is not possible to give the opposing counsel warning. If the opposing counsel is verbally prepared for what you are about to do, he or she is less likely to react and want to retaliate. Such personal communication also exudes confidence and builds trust. All experienced attorneys know that more can be accomplished with trust than distrust.

4. *Cooperate with opposing counsel.* In *Negotiate This!*, Cohen writes, "I believe it's always advisable to begin every negotiating encounter in a cooperative fashion."[2] Even Donald Trump agrees, stating, "Most negotiations should proceed calmly, rather than in a hostile manner."[3] Anyone who ever practices law for even a short time knows that a very high proportion of what lawyers do is negotiation. Therefore, always cooperate. For example, never schedule anything without making courteous arrangements with opposing counsel, unless to do so would be stupid (which is almost never). For example, if you need to schedule a motion to compel, call opposing counsel and tell him that if his client is unable to provide you with discovery, you will need to ask the court to resolve the dispute and arrange a hearing. If opposing counsel does not respond in a reasonable manner, then, of course, the hearing must be set. But considerable leeway should be provided, for many reasons. First, if you schedule something without prior consultation, you will make the opposing attorney angry and

he will look for ways to get you back. Second, opposing counsel will file a motion for continuance with the court and attempt to expose you to the court as someone who is uncivil in scheduling matters. Third, the court will likely give opposing counsel a continuance, and you will have wasted time pursuing the matter. Finally, by extending courtesy, you will be repaid—in most circumstances—with similar courtesy.

5. *Never argue.* Cohen states: "Never be confrontational, dogmatic, or abrasive. Express your point of view in a soft tone without hesitation."[4] Unfortunately, many lawyers view themselves as invincible warriors. They are waiting for the opportunity to fight, even if they are wrong—which they will never admit. Therefore, the most counterproductive step you can take with a lawyer is to argue with him. For example, a lawyer calls you and demands some unreasonable sum of alimony for his client. The normal reaction would be to say something like, "You've lost your mind if you think you can get that. There is no point in talking further settlement with you if you have that attitude." But that reaction will only lead to warfare or an end to settlement talks, at least until the judge forces negotiation on the day of trial. A better response might be: "Do you have some case law to support that position? If you do, please send it to me so I might reevaluate my position, as I certainly don't want to mislead my client as to what the law is."[5]

6. *Never humiliate.* Some years ago, I used to pick up my young daughter at her friend's house. One day, a little, white German shepherd puppy came out the door and barked at me. Thinking it would be funny, I barked back at it in a deep voice. He squealed and scurried back into the house. Every time I went to that house for weeks, I barked and the dog squealed and scurried back into the house. I thought that was pretty amusing. Months went by, and I returned to the home where the cowardly puppy lived. Without paying any attention, I got out of the car to open the door for my daughter. Out of the corner of my eye, I saw a white blur. Before I could tell what was happening, I realized that I was being bitten right on my butt by a *big* white German shepherd. The moral of the story: it does not matter who or what it is, or what its station in life, if you humiliate a living being, it will come back to bite you.

Techniques to Avoid Retaliation

Most anger and most mean actions by lawyers are the result of fear. So, when another lawyer does something mean or uncivil, ask yourself what they are afraid of. By the same token, when you have the urge to do something nasty or uncivil, ask yourself what *you* are afraid of. You are better off if your opponent is not afraid. So, do everything you can to put opposing counsel at ease and to engender trust. We have even developed what we call the civility letter. (A copy is reproduced in Appendix 9A.) We send this letter to opposing counsel at the start of each case in hopes of creating trusting cooperation.

When you want to retaliate, check yourself with a couple of techniques. The first technique is to remember that the lawyer you want to smash today may be a judge tomorrow! Another technique is the civility conference. Whenever a lawyer in your firm has a desire to retaliate by filing a nasty pleading or sending a nasty letter, make him call together at least two other members of the firm to discuss the matter. Almost always the planned action will be abandoned.

Different Personalities

All lawyers are different, so that you cannot define a "lawyer personality." Of course, many of us have a self-image of Atticus Finch as the ideal lawyer, but Atticus is fictional and I have yet to meet a real-life Atticus. Since we are all different, we must recognize our differences and not allow them to become sources of irritation or conflict. Below is a list of lawyer personalities that I have compiled over the years. When dealing with lawyers, remember that they are going to have one of the following personalities and that the way they treat you is probably not personal. More importantly, realize that you are not going to be able to change them.

1. *Bam Bam*—baby lawyers with their new big stick, the young lawyers aggressively trying to make a name for

themselves. They operate under the assumption that litigation is like a boxing match, and their objective is to knock the other lawyer's head off. They think it is fun.

2. *The Adolescent*—lawyers with about ten years of experience. These lawyers are just coming into their own and are feeling their power. They want people to know that they have arrived and are a force to be reckoned with. They know what to do, and they understand the force they have at their disposal. The problem is that they are like teenagers; they have the strength and attributes of adults but not the experience.

3. *The Advocate*—lawyers who believe the client is boss. These lawyers operate under the philosophy that people are paying them to be sons-of-bitches. They believe that the client is king and that they have the right to aggressive advocacy of their position, no matter what. These lawyers do not believe it is their place to try and counsel their client on the long-term consequences of their action or on the "right thing to do." These lawyers will assist a man in not paying child support.

4. *Rambo*—lawyers who have personal problems. These lawyers have anger in their hearts from personal history. Not knowing how to control their anger, they use it in an attempt to control results. Unfortunately, these lawyers are usually very smart and cunning.

5. *Albert Einstein* (this is not me)—good—usually very intelligent—lawyers who have little patience for what they regard as the inadequacies of the rest of us. They are going to teach the other lawyer a lesson. If the other lawyers do not promptly return telephone calls, they will strike in order to teach a lesson. If the other lawyers should dare to disagree with the Intellectual's decree as to the law in the case, the intellectual lawyers will penalize him.

6. *Oscar*—sloppy lawyers who do not have the training, ability, or interest in organizing their offices. They have work—sometimes a lot of it—and they believe that they are in the practice of law to help people, though they are not particularly intense about it. They do not charge a lot, and they take on little "causes." Unfortunately, they do not earn enough for their efforts to have the staff necessary to meet their volume of business. They find themselves in court all the time litigating. They usually believe the client is king but not in the truly dangerous way of the Advocate. Because of their disorganization, they do not return phone calls, they miss depositions, and they file things without thinking. They really do not intend to be uncivil but that is how it feels when you are on the other end of it.

7. *The White Knight*—lawyers who take their clients' causes personally and are on a mission to rescue them. These are generally good lawyers who think they are civil, but sometimes their rescue mission obscures their objectivity. They tend to attack with righteousness.

8. *The Southern Gentleman*—lawyers who think that as long as they are complete gentlemen they can do just about what they want. They are so very nice that the judges love them. When you are on the other side from such a lawyer, you find yourself "pulling punches" because you do not want to be uncivil to him, but when you do that, you are caught in his web. These lawyers will lead you to believe time after time that they are going to work with you, so you pull back, but the true cooperation you thought you were going to get never comes. The Southern Gentleman also has the capacity to court you like an old pal and then stick you right in the heart at the most unexpected time.

9. *El Destructo, the Bad Lawyer*—these lawyers simply do not know what they are doing. As a result they usually cause a lot of damage, even though they are

not winning. They are like the Chicago Bears of the late 1960s: they may not beat you, but when you are through with the game, half your team will be injured. Unfortunately, El Destructo shares many of Rambo's qualities but not the skill.

Abandon the Winning Mentality

One of the mentalities that creates a lack of civility is the concept that you have to "win" a case. Although this mentality may prove useful in other areas of law, it is destructive in family law. Over the years, I have run into countless lawyers who act like they are trying to beat me, or who are trying to prevent me from beating them. I have the impression that they think there is some giant scoreboard in the sky, which all can see, keeping score on which lawyers are "winning" and which lawyers are "losing." The public has bought into this scenario. I cannot tell you how many times a client has asked me, "What's your win/loss record against (the other lawyer)?"

Benjamin Sells, former litigator, now psychotherapist, discusses "winning" in *The Soul of the Law*:

> [When a lawyer attempts to win a case] he is mimicking conduct from a time when might literally made right. When the legal profession places winning over altruistic ideals, it is returning to its barbaric roots.
>
> The return of barbarism in the context of winner-take-all litigation endangers the very ends the legal mind seeks to ensure. If winning supplants idealism, then anarchy, the Law's Great Enemy, must follow as all sides do whatever is necessary to win. The argument that the quest for winning is proper as long as it is carried out "within the rules" is simply another way of saying the End is justified by the Means.[6]

The "winning" attitude hurts not only the greater good, according to Sells, but also the lawyer: "Can there be any doubt," Sells writes, "that such attitudes eat away at the lawyer, eroding the banks of morality?"[7]

If you do not buy the philosophical arguments against attempting to "win" family law matters, consider this: family law courts were established with the very notion of taking "winning" out of the equation. Family law courts are courts of *equity*. All of us are taught in the first years of law school that one must do *equity* to receive *equity*. Equity is about *fairness*, not winning.

Family law cases instruct us that a family law court expects a party to do the right thing *even* if the other side does not. Family law courts are not commissioned to pick a winner; they are commissioned to listen to the evidence and do the *fair* thing, given the law and the equities.

What this means is that you cannot "win." Even if you "outlawyer" the other side, the court's obligation is to do what is fair. The court is actually obligated to keep you from "winning" if the result is not fair. And if you should somehow win in the trial court, the appellate court will probably take the win away from you.

Another thing that happens when you try to beat someone and succeed is that the beaten party spends the rest of his or her life trying to even the score. Instead of producing an end to conflict between the parties, the beating produces continual post-divorce conflict. This is not in your clients' best interests.

The point is this: the family lawyer's real job is to assist the court in finding a fair result. If you try to do anything else, the court will not listen to you. Don't confuse this message with the notion that you are not supposed to diligently represent your client. That is not the point. The point is the focus of your efforts. The focus should be on presenting a fair and plausible position with fair and plausible requests for relief, instead of looking for ways to "win." The focus should be on meticulously gathering the facts and the law and presenting the case based on the law. The focus should be on making the judge's decision to go your way easy.

Once other lawyers understand that you are not trying to "beat them," then civility is restored. As long as other lawyers figure you are trying to beat them, they will be trying to beat you to the punch. Such a lifestyle is unhealthy for the lawyer and counterproductive for the client.

Notes

1. Cohen, Herb, *Negotiate This!*, p. 198 (New York: Warner Books, 2003).

2. Ibid., p. 88.

3. Trump, Donald, *How to Get Rich*, p. 116 (New York: Random House, 2004).

4. Cohen, *Negotiate This!*, p. 279.

5. Ibid., p. 227.

6. Sells, Benjamin, *The Soul of the Law*, p. 81 (Rockport, MA: Element, 1994).

7. Ibid.

Dealing with Clients, Part I

10

HOW MANY TIMES HAVE YOU HEARD A LAWYER say, "Law practice would be okay if it weren't for the clients"? Funny, no? Unfortunately, that is the way many lawyers feel. And is there any wonder? Many clients are difficult, and perhaps the most difficult are divorce clients. Walt Bachman makes the following observations about difficult clients:

> In the late-night conference rooms, at noisy bars, in living rooms with close colleagues, friends, and confidants, anywhere they kick off their shoes, loosen their ties, pull off their glasses and earrings, lawyers use one word more than any other to describe the type of clients who are all too present in any thriving practice these days. The likely subject of this epithet is the kind of client who can obsessively dominate one's waking thoughts and keep him or her up at night, invade a marriage for weeks on end, rule the lawyer's very existence, and generally cause trouble far out of proportion to the person's weight or worth. This word can be applied to the peevish incompetent client as well as to one who is darkly sinister. By informal consensus of usage,

no single term, scatological or not, better describes those people ultimately responsible for the explosion of litigation in our country over the last thirty years, who cause endless headaches for lawyers and everyone else in their vicinity. This one word most employed by lawyers to vent their feelings about their worst clients is "[difficult client]."[1]

Bachman estimates that 10 percent of the population are "[difficult clients]." But for litigation clients, even in elite firms, Bachman estimates that 40 percent of the litigants are in this category.[2]

Bachman's look at the nature of the litigation client is humorous, perhaps true, and certainly something we should always remember. If nothing else, it means we have a hard job.

There is plenty of reason to bend over backwards to make our difficult clients happy, primarily because unhappy clients will talk—they will talk all over town. According to most marketing experts, an unhappy client will tell up to twenty people how unhappy they were with you. In contrast, a happy client will tell only five to seven people.[3]

Be Careful Before You Act

Lawyers want to help people; most of us, in fact, entered the profession out of a desire to serve humanity. We all have a pretty good bit of the "White Knight" in us. We tend to listen to our client's side of the story and then jump on our white horse and ride into battle. Unfortunately, this can get us into a lot of trouble.

The worst thing a lawyer can do is accept his client's story without verification. Clients can and will mislead you for any one of a number of reasons, some intentional, some not. Either way, however, they will blame *you* if a mistake is made as a result. Always try to verify a client's story. A good example of this happened to me some years ago. I represented a woman who came to me because her husband left her. We looked at the finances and saw that he had been moving assets to his name over the last three years and had transferred a substantial amount of money out of an account just weeks before the separation. He left only a small amount in a joint account out of a very large estate. I told my client that she should take the money that was left because it looked like that was what her husband wanted her to have. Several days later, a female lawyer called me to say she represented the man and that she could not believe my bad faith in having my client take the last money out of the joint account. I said, "Well, did he tell you that *he* took all of the rest of the money just weeks ago?" "No. If he did, then that changes everything," she said. I said, "it certainly does." She called her client and then called me back and apologized.

Before you jump on your white horse and assume your client is a saint and the opposing party is a total villain, stop and ask yourself, "I wonder what the other side of the story is." This will help you assess your client's chances of success. For example, you have a female client who comes to you complaining that her husband had "beaten" her the night before. Questions should then be asked to verify this story, such as, "Did you call the police?" "Did you go to the doctor?" "Did you tell the doctor that he hit you?" Often, your client will not have called the police or gone to the doctor. Instead, your client will often have told the police or a doctor that her husband did not hit her; that she fell down the stairs. Now, this does not mean you do not have a valid abuse claim, but it does indicate that there may be trouble in proving it.

Or you might find out that an argument and alleged abuse took place in the house the night before because the husband just found out the wife was having an affair with the husband's best friend. Again, that does not necessarily mean that no abuse took place, but it certainly complicates the case.

Finally, remember that saints rarely marry devils. Although it may sound harsh, I find that frequently people deserve each other. That is, you should always assume there is no right and wrong on the story; that the other party can show a very plausible explanation or a mitigating circumstance. You have to be careful how you explore this issue with your client. It hurts your relationship with your client to say, "You don't expect me to believe that, do you?" Nor can you say, "Well, you must have done something to make him act like that." Instead, try this, "What will your husband say you have done to cause trouble in the marriage?" "What will your husband complain about, about you?"

The Lawyer as Counselor

Many theories on the obligation of the lawyer have been proposed. They range from the belief that legal representation should be completely client driven to the belief that it should be completely lawyer driven. Whatever your belief, lawyers have a role to *counsel* their clients, in addition to providing legal options and alternatives. In our field of family law, it is my opinion that we are absolutely obligated to counsel our clients to "do the right thing." Divorce courts are courts of "equity." Most of our family law decisions abound with concepts such as "you must come into court with clean hands" or "you must do equity to receive equity."

Wise lawyers soon learn to forsake the immediate opportunity to strike in favor of the prospect of positive, long-term constructive results. For example, a lawyer representing a man might have the opportunity to limit the amount of support paid by his client to a custodial mother. But if that opportunity is taken, what are the man's long-term prospects for enjoying maximum visitation with his children? If the man is hard on the woman in the divorce, she will most likely retaliate by making visitation difficult for the father. Unless the father does not care about seeing his children, lack of positive time with his children is not in either his or his children's long-term best interests. Good lawyers have the obligation to consider these long-term consequences in every decision they make.

Difficult People to Represent

Some people are more difficult to represent than others. Of course, one always gets into trouble when one puts people into groups, but these are the types of people who are tough to represent:

> *Women, or men, who have been abused over a long period of time.* When someone has been abused over a long period of time, they are firmly entrenched in the cycle of abuse. They are inextricably tied and bound to their

abuser. Years of therapy will be required to break the cycle. The lawyer cannot control this problem. These clients will shoot themselves *and your case* in the foot. For example, they will call you and complain that their spouse, from whom they are separated, has come over to the house and walked around in the house and cursed them. You will call the opposing counsel to complain and find out that your client *invited the spouse over to the house.* Worse, they sometimes go back to their spouse after you have obtained protective orders. Then, they get mad at you and will not pay your bill, even though you leapt to their defense on an emergency basis. I had a case many years ago where the husband was very abusive. I was in court on a hearing for a preliminary injunction and brought in pictures of busted kitchen cabinets, holes in the wall, and bruises on the face of my beautiful young client. I was in the courtroom, getting ready to get up on my white horse and slay the dragon for this damsel in distress, when the judge came into the courtroom and said, "Well, the situation must not be too bad, your client and her husband are in the hallway making out."

A mother who believes her child was abused by the father. There is no way to appease a mother who believes her young child has been abused by the father. There is no relief you can obtain from a court which will satisfy her. These mothers will be emotional and angry and on a mission. If you represent a client in this situation, be prepared for an unhappy ride, even if you think you did the best job possible.

Lawyers. Lawyers are very difficult to represent. First, they tend to want to play aggressive litigation games. They feel that since they are lawyers, they should be able to dominate the other side and control the court system. They also will get you to drop your normal attorney–client procedures and methods, because you assume they know what is going on and do not need the standard procedure. Wrong! Of course, they will play lawyer with you and tell you what to do and question your every move. Finally, they will challenge your bill or even not pay it. They may assume you should not charge them because they are a brother lawyer. When you represent a lawyer, watch it.

People referred by judges. Perhaps the highest accolade you can receive is to get a referral from a judge. The problem is that the person referred is usually trouble, for anyone seeking a referral from a judge is usually seeking an unfair advantage. They feel that if they ask a judge for a referral, they will get a lawyer who has an "in" with judges. They expect to get something they are not entitled to. These people expect a miracle.

People fearing retirement. People who have worked outside of the home and who are facing imminent retirement age are in a tough situation. They are very emotional and usually scared to death: they know retirement is near, but they are not used to the idea. This is unlike the person who has already reached retirement age and has thus had time to process and adjust to the idea.

Young women who want to fool around sexually. In a growing trend, women are interested in the night life and fooling around, in much the same way that many people have always assumed only men are. I mentioned this to a psychiatrist recently, and he indicated that women have always been this way, but I do not agree. The problem in representing these women is that they are so interested in just having fun that they will do absolutely stupid things that are destructive of their case. They will do so even though custody of their children is threatened.

Fighting for Principle

Sometimes you will get clients who have a difficult or expensive battle ahead, and you will advise them that it is probably not worth their while to go forward, but they want to anyway. And then they will utter the fateful words, "It's a matter of principle." Many times, this noble statement is accompanied by the expectation that they will pay you for this fight for principle when the matter is concluded. When someone asks you to fight for principle, quickly calculate in your head what the full legal tab for the cause might be, double it, and then tell the client you will be glad to go forward on the matter on two conditions: one, they understand that they are pursuing a cause they may not win, and two, they provide all of the fees in advance, so that they can be sure that the resources are there to do the job properly.

Dealing with Emotions

The hardest part of being a divorce lawyer is dealing with your own clients' emotions and personality flaws. Intense emotion is involved in any litigation but becomes multiplied in divorce or custody litigation. There are no clearcut ways to deal with these emotions. When you are dealing with human beings, sometimes there is no way to win. Here are some things to keep in mind.

"I Understand"

It is natural for people to be in pain while going through divorce. Communicate to your clients that you understand their pain; when they talk to you, say, "I understand your pain." Or say, "You have every right to be hurt, or mad." Validate their pain and their feelings. If their anger or pain turns to a desire for vengeance or retaliation, monitor this feeling closely and do not permit it to last.

Simply listen to your clients tell you of their pain without interrupting or giving a solution. When the new client comes in, simply say, "So, what's the matter?" This will make your clients feel that you care about what is happening to them and that they are not just a legal problem to be solved. It usually does not take more than twenty minutes for a client to tell their story, and then you can get the information you need for the legal advice.

Never Lose Patience

Never, never, lose patience with your clients. If you do, they will never forgive you. One caveat: Never losing patience should not be confused with failing to set appropriate boundaries. Boundaries must be set.

Coach Clients

Coach clients on how to deal with the fear and the anger they feel. Many clients are very afraid about what is going to happen to them, so coach them in the spiritual concept of "staying present." This means that they should not think about tomorrow but only what is facing them in the present. For example, a client has just been served with a lawsuit and is panicking. He is scared that his life will be turned upside down. Say something like this, "Don't worry, stay present. Nothing is going to happen today. Nothing is going to happen tomorrow. As a matter of fact, nothing is going to happen for a long, long time. We don't even have to respond to this for thirty days. So, just stay in the present and don't worry about tomorrow. There are a lot of things that have to happen and a lot of time to pass before it is even possible for anything to happen."

Many clients will engage in "catastrophe thinking." They will use strong negative language, such as "everything is going against us," or "they are always on the offensive and we are doing nothing," or "my life is ruined." When clients start to think or talk in this way, stop them and walk them through reality steps. For example, a female client whose husband had left her for another woman may say that her whole life is a disaster. You might respond with something like, "Well, I understand that you never dreamed you would be in this position, but is your whole life really a disaster? You have good health, right? You have three great children who are healthy and love you, right? You have a great family, who has come to your aid and support and shown you love in this trying time, right? Now, there are really a lot of great things going on in your life, aren't there?" When you pursue this type of systematic reality check, the person usually realizes they are overreacting. (See Chapter 7 for instruction on how to stop clients and yourself from catastrophizing.[4])

Warn Clients about Potential Problems

The first thing that an opposing party does when he finds out his spouse has a lawyer is to attempt to undermine that relationship.

He does so in order to to gain advantage in the proceedings. Warn clients beforehand, in the initial interview, that this is going to happen. Say, for example,

> Now, I want to warn you what your husband is going to say when he finds out that I represent you. He is going to try to undermine your relationship with me. He doesn't want you to trust me. He will try to make you lose faith in me. This happens all the time and I have learned to warn people about it. He is going to say something like, "Chinn is going to take all of your money," or "you've done it now, if you hadn't hired him, I would have taken care of you, but now, it's war," or "you must be sleeping with him." Trust me, he will say something like this. And when he does, you will be ready for it.

"My Spouse Will Pay Off the Judge"

Every family law lawyer will hear concerns that the opposing party is going to "pay off" the judge. The client will then tell the lawyer how unscrupulous and influential the other party is. The threat will often sound plausible. For years I worried about this possibility until I realized, "Hey, judges aren't supposed to do that, and there is no way I could know if they did, so there's no point in worrying about it." So, when a client tells you they are afraid the judge is going to be paid off, say something like this:

> Judges are sworn to uphold the law and decide cases fairly and without prejudice. That is their job. In all of my years of practice, I have never personally known a judge to have taken a bribe. We have good judges here. We must assume the judge will do what he is sworn to do.

Don't Badmouth the Judge or the Opposing Lawyer

It is often tempting to talk with your client about how bad the other lawyer is or how bad a judge is. Do not do this. Do not say things about opposing counsel or the judge which are judgmental or disrespectful. For example, do not tell your client, "That opposing counsel is a jerk to deal with, and he is going to take this case into the gutter." There are many reasons to refrain from such talk. First, there is a good chance your client will tell the opposing party, who will tell the opposing counsel. Second, when we talk in a judgmental fashion, it causes the client to lose a little faith in lawyers in general, because you have placed matters on a personal instead of a purely professional level. Finally, when we talk bad about opposing counsel and judges, it makes the client lose faith in the judicial system, which causes the client anxiety. Of course, this does not mean that you should paint a fairy tale picture of a judge or an opposing counsel when it is not true. On the contrary, you have an obligation to advise your client of the tactics an opponent may use, or the propensities a judge might have. But this can be done in a nonjudgmental or nonpersonal manner.

Set Boundaries

Setting boundaries is very difficult to do, for a fine line exists between understanding and caring and establishing a boundary. Hear are some points on setting boundaries:

The client cannot be allowed to be rude or abusive to staff. If she is rude, say something like, "I know you are having a hard time, but we need to have some ground rules in order to help you. You cannot be abusive to my staff, okay? If you do, we will have to make a change." If the client continues, the representation should be terminated.

The client must pay the bill. If he does not, say, "You have not paid our bill. Do you have some concern about our bill or our service? It is important to your representation that you provide sufficient resources for proper representation. Can I expect your check in the next few days?" If he does not pay, get out before the damage gets too great. If he is not trying to pay you, he does not respect you and will never pay you, no matter how hard you try to build points with him.

Clients cannot be permitted to remain too emotional for too long. If you have clients that simply cannot get control of their anger or hurt, then that is a danger sign that they have problems you are not qualified to handle. You should say something like this, "I understand you have been subjected to a horrible betrayal and that it has been very painful for you, but at some point we need to put the pain behind us and move forward. If you cannot, you have problems that our firm is not qualified to deal with."

Then, if the extreme emotion continues, the representation must be terminated, if possible.

Documentation

There are two basic schools of thought on the issue of documentation. One school says that you should document very little. That way, nothing can pin you down. The other school says that you should carefully document everything. This, of course, is what the medical community has started doing in the last forty or so years. I believe in carefully documenting every activity and every instruction.

Phone Calls

Every telephone call of every kind in a file should be documented in writing; this is true even for missed attempts. For example, I have had clients complain that I have not returned their telephone calls. I am able to show them where I have documented one or more phone calls to them with no answer. The easiest way to document telephone calls is to obtain a case management system. This system can automatically dial telephone numbers for you, automatically time the call, and provide a window for you to type a narrative of the discussion.

An added benefit of keeping contemporaneous notes of phone calls is that you can simply copy the notes and send them to the client for their information and save the time and money it would take to send them a letter. When you do this, type at the bottom of the phone notes: "I am sending a copy of these notes to the client so she will know what was discussed."

Letters and E-mail

Letters and e-mail should be used whenever possible to document discussions. A lawyer should never allow a verbal understanding to survive a minute without a written confirmation. For example, you talk to opposing counsel and agree to postpone a hearing to another date. The second you get off the phone, a letter or e-mail should be sent to the opposing counsel that says, "I am writing to confirm that you requested postponement of the hearing and you will notify the court administrator of the change of date." Another example: Your client tells you that she wants to put the litigation on hold because she and her husband are "talking." The second you get off of the phone, you write your client, "I am writing to confirm that you have instructed me to place your litigation on hold until further notice from you." I cannot tell you how many clients have told me to place litigation on hold and then a year later will complain to me that their case has taken over a year and still they do not have any legal result. The confirmation letter is a lifesaver in those situations.

Opinion Letters

The divorce business is very perilous because the results of negotiation or litigation in a divorce case are unpredictable. A client can take many different directions and make many different choices. We must operate our practices in a way that discloses to our clients the options available to them, the legal standards, and the consequences of each course of action. We should then cover our malpractice behinds by confirming the fact that the client has chosen a particular course of action and understands the consequences. We do this at critical intervals in the life of the file by sending a detailed "opinion letter." The letter usually states the facts as we understand them, the legal and other options available (e.g., sue for divorce, mediate, do nothing), the consequences and possible results of each course of action (e.g., suit will start litigation and possibly escalate animosity while mediation may save time and money but may result in loss of leverage due to trial), and the course of action chosen by the client (e.g., "You have chosen to file suit at this time and forego the opportunity to explore settlement through mediation").

Firing Clients

There comes a time in any business when a client must be fired. I have heard more than one experienced lawyer say, "I have fired more clients than I have kept." Clients must be fired in the following circumstances:

1. *They won't pay.* Clients who do not pay do not respect you. When the representation is over, they will file a bar complaint or malpractice claim against you. If clients do not pay their bill after repeated requests, fire them.

2. *They refuse to follow advice.* If clients do not follow your advice and things do not go well, they will still blame you. They will say, "You are the lawyer; you should have prevented me from doing that." If clients repeatedly fail to follow your advice, they are not benefiting from their relationship with you and should be given instruction to find a lawyer they trust enough to follow.

3. *They cannot control anger or grief.* If, over time, clients remain in an exaggerated or uncontrolled state of anger or grief, they must be terminated because sooner or later, you are going to become the target of their anger because you did not "fix it."

4. *They abuse staff.* A client is often willing to abuse the staff but acts like a pussy cat with the lawyer. The abuse of the staff is usually a harbinger of things to come for the lawyer. The abuser experiments with abusing the staff to see if you put up with it. If you do not take decisive action to stop the abuse of the staff, the abusive client then experiments with abusing you. The problem will not get better. The client must be fired.

5. *They are dishonest or immoral.* Obviously, if a client seeks to do something dishonest or immoral, they must be fired.

What to Say When Firing the Client

Say, "Mrs. Jones, the attorney–client relationship is a very important, trusting relationship. You are entitled to an attorney that you have faith in. I can tell that our relationship is not working well for you at this time, and it is in your best interests that I terminate my services to allow you to look for someone that you have confidence in."

When the Client Fires You

No matter what you do, whether you do your job right or whether you mess up in some way, you are going to be fired more than once in your career. Although it almost never feels good, it is something that must be accepted as part of the business. Your response to being fired depends on the circumstances. Sometimes the client really does not intend to fire you. A good lawyer usually has an instinct for this. When you have an instinct that your firing does not make sense or is not genuine, ask a few questions, such as, "I understand and respect your decision. Would you mind sharing with me why you have made this decision? Perhaps there is a misunderstanding that I can clear up." Sometimes this type of inquiry will lead to a discussion that will resolve the issue and lead to continuance of the relationship.

If the client's decision to terminate the relationship is firm, or if you believe the decision is a good one, be gracious and do not be offended by it. Above all, give the client immediate comfort that his wishes will be respected and that you will quickly make copies of his file for him. Respond by saying, "I understand and respect your decision. The attorney–client relationship is one where there must be great trust, and I want you to have that. I can assure you that our firm will work with you and your new counsel to get copies of the file to your new counsel and work with them to bring them up to speed on your case."

Transferring the file often leads to considerable strife, no matter what you do. It seems that terminating clients are just chomping at the bit to find you guilty of giving them a hard time in retrieving their file. This creates even greater tension when the termination takes place after you have entered an appearance with a court. The reason: you cannot stop the representation—even though fired—until the court releases you. Since clients never understand that, you must be very sensitive to this problem.

Many times a client will call one of your junior staff members and say, "I am firing your firm and I want to come by and pick up my file." Other times, they will send a short, terse letter: "I am terminating your services and will send a representative to retrieve my file." These clients are usually emotional and are just waiting for your firm to delay them or give them grief. Train your staff to remain calm and assure them that proper steps will be taken to get them a copy of their file, but some time may be required to accomplish the task. The staff member should then make sure that a responsible attorney is immediately notified.

Before handling one of these difficult situations, consult the ethics and decisions of your jurisdiction to determine exactly what your obligations are. Adopt the following procedure:

1. If the matter is in litigation, advise the client of the procedure that must be followed with the court system. He must be advised that even though he may have ended his relationship with you, you are still obligated to answer to the court until there is a proper order entered relieving you of responsibility, not only to the client, but to the court. Clients usually do not understand this.

2. The client should be advised and assured that she will be given a *copy* of her file as soon as it can reasonably be accomplished. The client should be offered the alternative of having the file delivered to a copying service, as long as she is willing to pay the copying service. The client is advised that your firm must retain an accurate copy of the file for future reference.

3. The file should be carefully reviewed by the responsible attorney to make sure the client is not provided with materials that should not be given to her, such as evidence held in trust, materials subject to a confidentiality order, or private firm notes.

4. The responsible attorney must determine what copies of materials the firm should retain. Most often, the firm retains all copies in order to ensure maxi-

mum malpractice protection. However, sometimes it is sufficient to release materials without keeping a copy.

5. If there has been a court appearance, care must be taken not to release any file materials without first having obtained an order of withdrawal.

6. The file must be transferred to the client or his attorney, and a detailed receipt must be obtained upon delivery. If the client instructs that the file be delivered to someone other than himself, such instruction must be documented in writing, signed by the client.

7. The client must be sent a termination letter, confirming the conclusion of responsibility.

8. New counsel must be contacted and offered advice and assistance in bringing them "up to speed." New counsel must be forwarded key deadlines in the future, just as a matter of courtesy.

(Appendix 10A contains a letter terminating representation.)

Notes

1. Bachman, Walt, *Law vs. Life*, p. 122 (New York: Four Directions Press, 1995).

2. Ibid., p. 123.

3. Bell, Chip R., and Ron Zemke, *Managing Knock Your Socks Off Service*, p. 45 (New York: AMACOM, 1992).

4. Kabat-Zinn, Jon, *Full Catastrophe Living* (New York: Dell Publishing, 1990).

Staff 11

THE FIRST DECISION TO MAKE regarding staff is whether to hire any at all. In the early stages of practice, or when you do not have sufficient resources to hire staff, it is appropriate to manage your office without hiring someone. With the use of computers and phone messaging systems, attorneys can operate rather nicely without staff assistance. The first two key services provided by staff are document preparation and telephone answering. These tasks can now be performed with technology, thus eliminating the need to hire someone. The technology available at our desktop allows us to communicate by e-mail or fax anywhere in the world without ever leaving our desk. An attorney who learns how to type or use voice command software does not need a secretary to prepare or send a document. Document merger programs allow the attorney to quickly generate pleadings and other lengthy documents without an inordinate amount of typing. Phone message systems can be utilized to answer the phone and relay messages to the attorney through voice mail.

Contract Labor

Attorneys who need some secretarial or paralegal support can avoid hiring a full-time employee by utilizing contract labor. For example, many people like to perform contract labor instead of becoming employees. Often persons wish to work only part time. In the first year of my practice, I did not hire a secretary, but I needed someone to generate documents for me. I paid a secretary from the law firm of friend of mine to pick up my dictation every afternoon and return it to me the following day. I paid her by the page. This relationship was beneficial to both of us. She earned extra money, and I got my typing done without obligating myself to a full-time or even part-time employment relationship. Contract or part-time labor can be found through friends or acquaintances or through employment agencies.

The Decision to Hire Staff

Probably nothing is more important to the success of a law firm—or any other business for that matter—than the hiring of staff. Nothing will cause you more consternation, grief, and damage than staff problems. You will lose more sleep and have more stress over staff problems than over client problems. Great care, then, must be taken in hiring and training staff. People are your number one asset.[1] The foundation of a great firm is the way it develops people. Great leaders must commit as much as 40 percent of their time to selecting, appraising, and developing people.[2]

Hire Good People

I once heard that legendary Alabama football coach Bear Bryant told another coach, "I can beat you with my players or I can beat you using your players." I was always impressed with that and had fantasies that I could be that kind of boss; that I could take anyone and train that person to be a great employee. WRONG. There is no set of incentives, no training, no reward system, no salary structure or benefit package that will transform bad people into good employees, or turn even mediocre people into good employees. This message was confirmed in Jim Collins's excellent book, *Good to Great*, which emphasizes the need to hire good people before doing anything else: "when in doubt," he said, "don't hire—keep looking."[3] Choosing the right people is what creates that elusive sustainable competitive advantage.[4] Even Donald Trump has weighed in on this subject, stating that you should "get the best people you can."[5]

What to Look For

The two basic components of a prospective employee are attitude and ability. The optimum employee has both good attitude *and* ability. Look *first* for attitude. If a person does not have the right attitude, there is nothing you can do. Look for whether the person has the willingness to adhere to the core values of your firm.[6] Look for energy and enthusiasm of execution. Does the person talk about the thrill of getting things done?[7]

Employment Interviews

You should observe the following simple techniques for hiring.

First, respect your first impression. If the prospect does not impress you right away, she is probably not the right choice. You must respect your first impression because that is a likely indicator of the impression the prospect will give others. For example, if, when you meet the prospect, he looks down, shuffles his feet, and gives you a weak handshake, take note; it is important.

Second, do not *rely* on your first impression absolutely. Just because someone looks and acts right in the initial interview, it does not mean they are right for you. Do not hire on the basis of instinct or impulse. Take your time.

Third, the biggest mistake lawyers make in interviewing employees is that they talk about themselves and their firm and what they are looking for instead of making the prospect talk. To find out if the prospect matches your firm, encourage her to talk before she knows what you are really about or what you are looking for. This is the only way to discover her true feelings.

Understand that prospective employees are trying to persuade you to hire them. Carefully craft questions that will reveal attitudes and viewpoints that are important to you. For example, instead of asking an employee if he is a hard worker, ask him: "What is a good day at work for you?" If he answers that it is a day when he works really hard, you might have an honest answer.

Fourth, use trusted, existing staff to help you. Not too long ago, I was talking with my staff about some past employees who had been fired. Two of my paralegals, who had been with me for several years, said, "If you just had *asked* us, we would have told you that every one of them wouldn't make it here. We can tell right away!" I said, "Okay, you have just made yourself a part of my hiring process." I now have a three-stage interview process: the first is the initial interview with me; the second is the interview with my entire staff; and the third is the final interview with me again. Our firm does not hire anyone who does not receive unanimous acceptance from the entire staff.

If you want to take steps in addition to interviews, you can take the prospect to lunch, or for drinks, or you can invite the prospect and spouse to dinner. Interviewing the prospect in nonoffice settings can reveal a lot about the true personality.

Check References

I am amazed at the hiring practices of law firms. I have had many, many employees leave my firm and go on to work for firm after firm in the following years, and not one law firm called me to find out about any employee's service record and attitude. If you want to have a reliable hiring process, you must ask for the names of every single prior employer of the candidate and then interview them. And make sure you talk directly to the person who supervised the candidate. This will take a lot of time, but you cannot spend too much time on obtaining and developing the best people.[8]

Hiring

The final step before hiring is to communicate the firm values to the prospect and obtain her commitment to them. Draft a list of firm values and an employee commitment sheet. The employee commitment sheet lists all of the things you expect out of an employee, such as the time of arrival, moral values, the time to show up early for court, the fact that clients should never wait, and the fact that fellow employees should be supported. (Such commitment sheets for attorneys and support staff are presented in Appendices 11A and 11B.)

Training

Many lawyers hire people and then stick them in an office and expect them to morph into knowledgeable employees. This is a recipe for creating unhappy and incompetent employees. Here are some key things you should do to train your new hires.

1. *Create a training and indoctrination checklist.* New hires must learn many things about the office, including office hours, word processing, billing policies, filing systems, work hours and holidays, and office procedures for everything from mail to staff meetings. Sit down with a key staff member or two and make up a checklist of the things that should be taught to the new hire before he or she ever starts work. Then schedule the new hire for an indoctrination session before the first day of work.

2. *Create and emphasize a list of firm values and expectations.* Your firm should have written values and standards for performance. These values should be emphasized in the hiring interviews, and they should be driven home upon hiring by having the new hire sign a written commitment to follow the firm's values and standards. In *The Game of Work*, Charles Coon-

radt states: "Missed or unfulfilled expectations are the number one cause of relationship failure. It is therefore imperative, from the very beginning, that you form the clearest possible expectations for an employee."[9] (Appendix 11C contains a sample values and standards statement.)

3. *Spend time with the new hire at the outset.* The firm leader should spend as much time as possible with the new hire at the beginning. As Coonradt says, "Don't let them out of your sight for the first forty-eight hours. Take them to lunch. Don't even let them go to the restroom unless you know they will be alone in there."[10] The reason is that the leader must convey the firm values and standards. Training in these matters cannot usually be delegated. In fact, it can be very dangerous to the firm's morale to allow anyone other than the most trusted of people (if not yourself) to indoctrinate a new hire. If you are going to hire someone, make sure you are willing to make an immediate time commitment to their indoctrination.

4. *Script critical matters.* Where possible, write a script for new hires to follow in certain circumstances. For example, write a script for your receptionist to follow when talking to people on the phone. She should know exactly what you want said in all critical situations. For example, I do not want my receptionist to tell people, "He hasn't made it in yet" when a call comes in before I arrive in the morning. I have therefore scripted what I want her to say.

Coaching

As managers in today's business environment, we must learn how to gently guide our staff to learn what they need to learn to perform properly. We must learn to be teachers who want all of our students to get A's.[11] If we feel we must get mad, or yell, or lose our temper, or act in a judgmental way, we must answer for ourself the following two questions: (1) do I need to learn how to manage better? or (2) do I have a person on my staff who does not belong in my firm?

The number one rule to follow is to treat your staff as though they are the children of a very influential person who will damage you if you hurt or insult them. That way, you will always treat them with the great care they deserve. Here are some specific guidelines:

1. *Never get angry.* If you are angry, something is wrong. It means that *you* have an issue, such as stress or fear, or something is wrong in your personal life. Or it may mean that the person you are angry with does not belong on your staff. Either way, getting angry with the staff member is not the way to handle it.

2. *Never yell or curse.* Yelling and cursing convey a lack of control. A supervisor should not convey to his staff that he has lost control.

3. *Never be judgmental.* No one likes to be judged. Judgment creates emotion in both the person being judged and the person doing the judging. This emotion interferes with performance, making the person who is judged resentful. Donald Trump says, "it will always work against you to demoralize your employees in any way."[12] "To belittle someone is to be little."[13]

4. *Coach in person.* No one likes to be reprimanded or criticized in writing or through e-mail or even an inner office "stickie." Uniformly, the receiver gets the writing, reads it, and gets hurt or angry. This happens even if the note was totally innocuous. Therefore, always coach your people in person.

5. *Never say, "You are a good employee, but. . . ."* This phrase conveys judgment. Anyone who has ever heard that phrase knows they are about to be zinged. In an interesting treatise called *Management of the Absurd*, Richard Eason states that complimenting people actually may not be motivational because "praise is an evaluation, and to be evaluated is to be judged."[14]

6. *Think before you act.* I cannot tell you how many times I have seen a situation in my office and reacted by yelling at a staff member, only to hear that the matter was carried out at my instructions (which I had forgotten). The moral: slow down and take your time before you jump at someone in your office.

7. *Stay positive and keep your sense of humor.* If you have hired the right people, that is, people with the same values and work ethic you espouse, the last thing they would want to do is disappoint you. More than likely, they are absolutely busting their butts to please you. So stay positive with them at all times. Look for ways to convey your viewpoint with humor. Make it fun. Remember, when you are trying as hard as you can for a client, how much do you like it if they criticize you? You do not like it. You hate it, and sometimes you react by determining that you are not going to work as hard for them anymore if that is the way they are going to act. If the employees do not share your work ethic and values, you have made a bad hire.

8. *Give constant positive feedback.* We are all so attuned to making sure that mistakes are not made that we rarely give attention to noticing when things are done right. When things are done right, we are not good about giving positive feedback. "Most people don't understand the terrible feeling that getting no feedback produces."[15]

Quarterly Reviews

Conduct performance reviews every three or four months. "Quarterly reviews help keep plans up to date and reinforce synchronization. They also give the leader a good idea about which people are on top of their businesses, which ones aren't, and what the latter need to do."[16] These reviews must be very short, or you are unlikely to do them. The reviews should cover the following topics:

Production
Collections
Problems with performance
Employee complaints or needs
Successes
Lessons learned

Note the reviews on your calendar as though they were an appointment. Calendar them a long time in advance. If you do not, you will either bump the review for something you would rather do, or you will forget to do it.

Make it clear that raises are not a topic for quarterly reviews, or most assuredly, the employees will expect one.

Annual Assessments

Hold anniversary reviews with each employee as close to the actual day of their first day of employment as possible. Employees are programmed to think in terms of a raise at least once a year. Thus, if you do not meet with them and give them a raise once a year, they will grow resentful.

Annual assessments should be longer than quarterly assessments. The points that can be covered in annual assessments are as follows:

Production
Review of the firm mission and how the employee is help-
    ing the firm with that mission
Review of the employee's personal goals and how the
    firm is helping the employee meet his or her goals
Performance on cases
Cooperation with associates and staff
Bar work
Writing and speaking
Getting business
Professional development
Good qualities
Matters needing improvement
Formulation of goals for the coming year

Appendix 11D contains an annual assessment worksheet used in our firm. You may also consult the ABA publication *The Essential Form Book: Comprehensive Management Tools for Lawyers*, Volume II (2001) for more information on employee reviews.

Firing

The biggest lesson you must learn about supervising personnel is that once you get the feeling someone is not going to work out, you should nip the problem in the bud and fire him. Does that sound harsh? Well, it really is not, for you are not doing anybody any favor by keeping them on in a place where they are not happy. If they were happy, they would not be a problem.

The following passage from *Good to Great* accurately presents the principle of moving quickly to remove staff who are not performing properly:

> The moment you feel the need to tightly manage someone, you've made a hiring mistake. The best people don't need to be managed. Guided, taught, led—yes. But not tightly managed. We've all experienced or observed the following scenario. We have a wrong person on the bus and we know it. Yet we wait, we delay, we try alternatives, we give a third and fourth chance, we hope that the situation will improve, we invest time in trying to properly manage the person, we build little systems to compensate for his shortcomings, and so forth. But the situation doesn't improve.[17]

How to Fire

Before taking any employment action, consult with the laws of your state and with a labor lawyer. If you operate in an "employment at will" state, you may terminate employees for any reason at any time, except for discriminatory reasons. If you are dealing with someone in a protected group (age, gender, race, religion, etc.), consult with a labor lawyer.

Even though you can fire someone at any time, for any reason, it is best to follow a procedure of reprimand and warning. Written reprimands do not particularly engender employee loyalty or promote morale. Therefore, save the written reprimands for someone who clearly appears to be "on the way out." Written reprimands create a paper trail that may assist you when it comes to suit, unemployment compensation claims, and accusations of unfairness.

A reprimand should state what the employee did wrong, why the conduct is wrong, what needs to be done to correct it, and by when. If a repeat of the offense will result in termination, the reprimand should so state. The penalty for violating a firm rule or standard of employment should match the offense. For example, being late for work should probably not result in termination, but being late for court might. Another example is that being late for work once or twice might not result in termination, but being late again after two reprimands for being late might be grounds for termination.

When you reach the point of termination, two basic procedures are put in place. The first procedure is for people you do not think will attempt to damage the firm when told of their termination. The second procedure is for people who cannot be trusted. Many businesses believe they must function as though all terminated employees cannot be trusted. This philosophy guarantees that the terminated employees will not have access to the firm's computers or premises to do damage; it also guarantees that ill will be created in *all* terminated employees.

For employees who will not damage the firm, the termination could result in allowing the employee to remain on staff for a specified term in order to close projects, or continue earning money until another job can be found. This employee may be someone you really like but who has just not been able to perform to the firm's standards.

The second procedure is designed to protect the firm from damage. Here is how you do it: while you are conducting the conference to fire the employee, send another staff member to the terminated employee's office to lock the terminated employee out of the firm computer system. When the terminated employee returns to his office, the staff member assists the terminated employee in packing his materials. The terminated employee is escorted from the premises. This procedure is necessary to prevent the terminated employee from copying firm materials, throwing away or destroying client papers or evidence, stealing files, client lists, or materials, and doing something to damage the computer system. Upon termination, someone from the firm should contact key clients and advise them of the termination and assure the clients that there will be no interruption in their service. The clients must not hear of the termination from the terminated employee.

Whether following the first or second procedure, the conversation with the terminated employee is pretty much the same: "Joe, it has become evident that you do not fit in here at this firm. Your performance indicates that you must not be happy here and that you would be better off somewhere else. It is best for you that we terminate our relationship." No more really needs to be said.

Upon termination, it is important to obtain keys and firm property from the employee. If they walk out the door with something, it is not coming back. Our firm has installed an electronic key pad with a code number so that we can simply change the access code to the office upon someone's termination. We do this regardless of the nature of our relationship with the departing employee, because you never know what friend or family member they gave the code to.

You may read articles and books that talk about positive ways to deal with departing or terminated employees. These materials discuss the special companies that handle things in such a way that they have no enemies in former employees and how they actually become future allies of the firm. This may be possible, but most terminated employees are like jilted lovers. There are going to be latent resentments and anger, even in situations where the employee left of his own will and you urged him not to leave. Recognize that one of the things you cannot do anything about is the way people who leave your firm think of you. Do not fret over keeping a good relationship; just be businesslike and brief.

It is very important to not play games with pay, benefits, or pensions with a departing employee. Go to great lengths to treat them with fairness and decency. Make sure they get every nickel they are entitled to. Otherwise, you might get a visit from the Department of Labor. Err on the side of giving them more than you want to. However, there are no laws or rules requiring a severance package, and you should not feel any obligation to pay for such a package, unless you have a very high regard for the employee. Naturally, if you are going to pay any kind of severance, obtain a release for any and all claims in exchange. When you issue the final pay to the terminated employee, make a note on the check that the check is being negotiated in full settlement of all claims to wages by the employee.

Confirm the Firing in Writing

Just as you should document everything in regard to client matters, you should also document all of your dealings with your staff. When an employee is terminated, document the termination in writing, stating the reason for the termination and the date it occurred. This may be important for protecting the firm from Equal Employment Opportunity Commission (EEOC) or unemployment compensation claims. Never state a reason that is different from the actual reason. For example, you have terminated the employee for being habitually tardy, but you do not want to leave the employee with a bad employment record, so you state that you are terminating the employee for lack of business. The employee will take advantage of you and file a claim. When you try to contend the employee was fired for "cause," you will be impeached with your own letter.

Advise the employee of important rights and obligations, such as the obligation to elect COBRA coverage in writing within thirty days. (Attached as Appendix 11E is a sample termination letter.)

The ABA Law Practice Management Section has published *Handling Personnel Issues in the Law Office*, by Francis T. Coleman and Douglas E. Rosenfeld. Purchase that publication for assistance in personnel issues.

Flex Time

Under "flex time" employees have the right to work hours that are different from the standard work hours. Flex time can benefit both the firm and the employee. The benefits to the employee are obvious: they work when they want to. The firm benefits in a couple of ways. First, by allowing flex time, the firm may be able to keep a valued employee. Second, the firm obtains valuable assistance, without paying for a full-time employee.

The downside to flex time is that there are times when you need the flex employees and they are not there. For me, I can never keep track of their schedules, so I stay in somewhat of a state of confusion. But I want to keep the employees and so I put up with it.

Time Clocks and the Like

A few years ago, I was having trouble keeping track of employees arriving on time or leaving early. I was also having trouble keeping track of sick days and vacation days. Therefore I came up with the grand idea of a time clock. I installed it in the employee lounge and the employees were required to punch time cards. Well, that grand experiment lasted about a week. My advice: if you have trouble with tardiness or days off, you have an employee who needs to be someone else's employee. Give him a written warning or two, and then show him the door.

Procedures Manual

Many management books and labor authorities recommend that you create an employment manual that spells out the operations and rules of the office, disciplinary matters, vacation and sick pay benefits, health insurance, pension benefits, and so on. There are some things to remember about such manuals. Once a benefit or procedure or rule is put down in writing, it can become a legal obligation of the firm. If you create a manual, you should be careful to know what is in it and apply it. See *Law Office Procedures Manual for Solos and Small Firms*, 3rd ed., by Demetrius Pimitriou (ABA, 2005).

Delegation

If you are going to have employees, you must learn to delegate. Delegating is not easy, and lawyers have more trouble with it than any other profession. Lawyers generally feel that legal advice is a personal art and that no one can do it quite like they can. To an extent, that may be true, but any experienced lawyer knows that much of what we do is standard and mundane. I submit that 99 percent of what we do can be delegated, if done properly.

Delegation is an art that requires the same skill as effective law practice. Delegating does not mean just giving other people your work. In the early years of my firm, I thought I was doing a good job of managing when I gave my associates cases or projects and left them alone to perform their work. I was very wrong. I found they were often starving for direction and needy of time with me. They also did not perform as well as they could have and burned out after a couple of years. Reacting to giving too little supervision, I began to oversupervise. I took work back. I told people exactly how to do things and insisted they not deviate. This, of course, led to a revolt and to accusations of micro managing. I have now slightly corrected my management technique. I still insist that matters be done "my way," but I am careful never to criticize, and I ask what others think before telling them what I think, if I do at all.

The art of delegation requires the following elements:

1. Pick the right person for the job. Give assignments to people who want to do the work and who have the proper training and skill for it.
2. Give assignments in writing. The instructions should be very clear. Good employees want to know exactly what is required of them so that they can please you by doing it.
3. Define success for the job.
4. Create a definite and reasonable time limit.
5. Make sure you know exactly what you are doing. If you are delegating something you do not know how to do, look out!

6. Check on the progress of the assignment in appropriate ways without bothering the employees or making them think you do not have confidence in them. But you must check.

7. If the assignment is done correctly, praise the employee publicly. If it is not done right, privately tutor the employee on improvement. Never get angry. Never take failure of the employee personally. Never criticize in public. Always give feedback in person.

If you want to read something quick on delegation, pick up *The One Minute Manager*.[18]

Games and Awards

Use games to inspire the right conduct in your employees. In *The Game of Work*, Coonradt talks about how much enthusiasm, effort, and sacrifice human beings put into games *when there is usually nothing at stake other than a winning score*.[19] This book is dedicated to showing employers how to create the same energy in the workplace by the use of games. Our firm has employed games to encourage production and good service and to foster firm values. If you want to use games, think of the one thing you would most like to encourage in your office. Then see if you can create a game around it. You might want to involve your employees in the design of the game *and* the reward. The first game I ever used is "the service game." I picked the service game because that is the point that I want to emphasize the most in my office. The game is really quite simple. If I receive an unsolicited comment from anyone outside of the office that a member or members of my team provided unparalleled service, I announce the comment to the entire staff. The winner is given a crisp $20 bill. Now, who does not want a $20 bill? And, importantly, each of the rest of the members of the team gets a $5 bill. My point is to help the team see and experience the fact that everyone wins through one member's excellence.

Another game we play is a values awards game. We pick five values that we want to encourage in our team: teamwork, corporate athleticism, service, excellence, and spirit. The first time the awards were given, I gave them out. After that, the person winning the award picks the next winner. The award is $5 as well as recognition in the docket meeting. Is everyone happy to be recognized and get the $5? You bet. I even enjoy it when I win, and it is *my* $5 that I get. The team values awards are given each week. The spirit that is encouraged by team members recognizing each other is phenomenal.[20]

Encourage Healthy Habits and Good Values

Any one who works quickly realizes that most waking hours are spent at work with coworkers, not the family. Therefore, the workplace should become a wonderful, happy, nurturing environment. It is also common knowledge that people perform better when they are healthy and happy. Look for ways to encourage employee health and happiness. Here are some techniques:

Talk about health. Incorporate discussions about health in your everyday conversations. Talk about diet and exercise and healthy habits.

Give employees personal time. It is tough to take care of the necessities of life when you are always working during business hours. Consider giving staff regular or random time off during the work week to take care of personal matters.

Schedule fruit breaks. Jim Loehr and Tony Schwartz's *The Power of Full Engagement* talks about performance.[21] In one chapter, they discuss the fact that the human mind and body cannot concentrate on a subject more than 90 to 100 minutes at a time. They also discuss the body's need for nourishment about six times a day. Consider scheduling a health food break in the midmorning and midafternoon. This can be a time of mental and physical replenishment.

Create health contests or games. Create a contest for who can walk the most miles or stick to a healty eating plan or give up a vice.

Create firm workouts. Our firm has a weight room. The firm pays a trainer to come to the firm in afternoons to help the team members work out.

Exhibit healthy habits. Practice what you preach. If you believe that caffeine is bad for you, as I do, consider advising the staff that the firm will not provide coffee, Cokes, and so on, for the staff.

Give compliment parties. Every once in awhile, gather the team together and have them write out a short note as to what they like about every other member of the team. Throw the notes in a hat and then read them to the entire team. We did this not too long ago. The team enjoyed it so much that one of our industrious team members had the sayings placed on placards and gave them to all the employees to hang in their offices.

The Huddle

In football, the teams huddle before every play. The huddle is designed to bring everyone together for a few seconds to find out what everybody is supposed to do. Many teams hold hands in the huddle, and all teams "break" the huddle with a clap and a unison cry, such as "break." So, the huddle is also a morale booster for the team. You can accomplish the same things with a "huddle" in your office. Simply pick an appropriate time and walk down the hall and holler, "huddle up." Everyone will come out of their office for a minute. There, in the huddle, you can discuss a case or two, or an impending trial, or an issue of team spirit or morale. The beauty of the huddle is that it does not take long and it brings everyone together.

Notes

1. Martin, Linda, *Fail-Safe Leadership*, p. 83 (Orlando, FL: Delta Books, 2001).

2. Bossidy, Larry, and Ram Charan, *Execution, the Discipline of Getting Things Done*, p. 118 (New York: Crown Business, 2002).

3. Collins, Jim, *Good to Great*, p. 63 (New York: HarperCollins, 2001).

4. Bossidy and Charan, *Execution*, p. 110.

5. Trump, Donald, *How to Get Rich*, p. 4 (New York: Random House, 2004).

6. Martin, Linda, *Fail-Safe Leadership*, p. 113 (Orlando, FL: Delta Books, 2001).

7. Bossidy and Charan, *Execution,* p. 129.

8. Ibid., p. 130.

9. Coonradt, Charles A., *The Game of Work*, p. 115 (Park City, UT: The Game of Work, 1991).

10. Ibid., p. 116.

11. Blanchard, Ken, Bill Hybels, and Phil Hodges, *Leadership by the Book*, p. 149 (New York: William Morrow and Company, 1999).

12. Trump, *How to Get Rich*, p. 30.

13. Fox, Jeffrey J., *How to Become a Great Boss*, p. 102 (New York: Hyperion, 2002).

14. Eason, Richard, *Management of the Absurd*, p. 65 (New York: Touchstone, 1996).

15. Connellan, Tom, *Inside the Magic Kingdom*, p. 93 (Austin, TX: Bard Press, 1997).

16. Bossidy and Charan, *Execution*, p. 258.

17. Collins, *Good to Great*, p. 56.

18. Blanchard, Kenneth, *The One Minute Manager* (New York: William Morrow and Company, 1983).

19. Coonradt, *The Game of Work*, pp. 1–9.

20. Nelson, Bo, *1001 Ways to Reward Employees* (New York: Workman Publishing, 1994).

21. Loehr, Jim, and Tony Schwartz, *The Power of Full Engagement* (New York: Free Press, 2003).

Service 12

LAWYERS RARELY TALK IN TERMS OF SERVICE; instead, they focus on delivery of a legal product. Law schools give no classes on service, which is odd, for what business can survive without a fixation on service? Lawyers should refocus their attention on service. We will start with a description of the terminology we use and the way we evaluate our cases.

Did you ever wonder why clients are called *clients* instead of *customers*? I'm sure there is a valid reason, but I think that use of the term *client* instead of *customer* throws lawyers off of a service-oriented attitude. So, I encourage you to incorporate the word *customer* in your vocabulary to help you reprogram your brain toward service.

Monitor Results That Are Important to the Client

When you discuss the progress of a case, ask yourself and the staff, "Is the client (customer) happy?" For example, my associate is reporting to me on the results of a temporary hearing and is saying how the result achieved was within the range of desired results. After examining the results and our firm's actions, I might ask the question, "Is the client happy?" This is an important question, because both attorneys and reasonable clients know that a perfect result is rarely, if ever possible. Therefore, client satisfaction with the result is the final arbiter of a satisfactory result for the client. If the answer is that the client is not happy, then it is appropriate to immediately go into action to address the client's concerns and to educate the client about the reasonable results that could have been achieved. If the client remains unhappy, then that may be a signal that the relationship should be terminated. It is imperative in customer service to be constantly asking, "Is the client happy?' and immediately responding if the client is not happy.

Screening

The first service opportunity takes place in the initial communications with the client. First, the attorney and client should make sure that they are a proper fit; otherwise there will be less opportunity to deliver outstanding service. Another key element to providing high-level service is to talk about fees in the prospective client's initial contact with your office. Good business practice calls for you to advise the client of your fees in this initial contact. Fees thus become part of the screening process for both you and the client. Use a "screening" sheet that contains a list of the matters to be discussed in the screening call. At the bottom of this sheet, list your fees, or your hourly rates and your retainer. Tell the client what to expect regarding fees and make it clear that there will be a fee for the initial interview. This is important for many reasons. First, every firm has certain expectations about being paid. So does the client. It is important to match the client and the firm's expectations before any work is done or any money is spent. This reduces misunderstandings.

The Initial Interview

It is said that the first five minutes of the first interview are the most critical to creating the trust necessary to create a solid long-term relationship. Therefore, great care must be taken to make the initial interview work for attorney *and* client.

The initial interview begins as the client pulls into the parking lot. Is your office parking convenient? If not, look for ways to make it so. Your clients must feel that you are making a great accommodation for them and must feel comfortable visiting you. Is your parking lot clean and attractive?

The Receptionist

The heartbeat of customer service is the receptionist: this is where service starts and usually ends. Therefore, great care should be taken in hiring and training a receptionist. Your receptionist should appear, dress, sound, act, and talk in a manner that is completely consistent with the image you wish your firm to portray. The same is probably true for all employees, but it is critical for the receptionist.

The receptionist should not be smoking cigarettes, munching on fast food, reading a book, or playing cards on the computer. He or she should convey professionalism at all times and should speak clearly and in a professional way.

Create a script for your receptionist. Write what you want said and what you do not want said. For example, as noted earlier, if a client should call in the morning before an attorney arrives, the receptionist is instructed not to say, "He hasn't made it in yet" (which implies that the receptionist is annoyed she had to get up and get into the office, but the big shot attorney didn't). Or if a client should call late in the afternoon after an attorney has left, the receptionist is instructed not to say, "He's gone for the day" (which implies that the dirty so-and-so lawyer left early but left me here working).

When clients enter the reception area, the receptionist should stand and greet them as though their arrival had been greatly anticipated, much the same way one might anxiously await the arrival of a friend at your home. The receptionist should then say, "He is expecting you, I will tell him you are here. Would you like a cup of coffee or tea, or Coke?"

Reception Room

Much thought and effort should be put into the waiting area because this is the client's first impression of the office itself. As with everything that you do, design the reception area in a manner that is consistent with the mission of your firm and the clients you serve. For an extreme example, a lawyer who specializes in workman's compensation who is visited by construction workers or steel workers might have a different reception than a high-asset divorce lawyer. Construction workers, who have mud on their boots and dirt on their jeans, would feel less comfortable entering a posh environment. On the other hand, a lawyer who seeks the representation of wealthy people would want to create an environment that might be similar to a wealthy person's living room, an environment that commands a high fee.

The reception area should always be neat. There should be no clutter, no dirty cups or glasses, no papers or files lying about. Magazines should be maintained at all times in neat stacks. Here are some tips to help you create a great reception area:

Fine furniture
Artwork
Fountains
Aquariums
Fresh flowers
Candles
Potpourri
Statues
Historical photographs
Mementoes
Music

The selection of magazines should be designed to interest the customers. The selection should be kept current.

Do Not Let Clients Wait

Be prompt; excellent service requires that we not let our clients wait. I know that when I go to a professional, such as my CPA, I do not want to wait. I expect him to view me and my appointment as important and to meet me upon my arrival. Our clients expect the same. Make it a rule for yourself and everyone in your office that clients will not wait. If a client arrives and you are in the middle of crafting some brilliant language in a letter or brief, *stop* and work on it later. Resist the urge to finish your thought. If you are on a telephone call, tell the person you are talking to that you have to get off the phone because you have an appointment.

You can take certain measures to avoid making clients wait. First, do not schedule appointments too close together. For example, do not schedule one client at 10:00 A.M. and another at 11:00. Also, do not schedule client appointments at the beginning of office hours or at 1:00 P.M. because the client may beat you to the appointment. Do not try to squeeze in one last call before your appointment, because almost invariably the conversation takes much longer than expected.

If it is inevitable that your client has to wait for you, walk to the reception area and explain to the client that you got delayed and need just a minute before you can begin the appointment. If you cannot do this, have a staff member do it.

Go Get the Client

The lawyer should go to the reception area to greet the client. The client should not be told where to go or be led down a maze of hallways. And the lawyer should greet the client in reception. This makes the client feel special.

The Greeting

There is no one right way to greet a client. Some lawyers have their staff escort the client to their office or meeting room. This is probably okay. But I prefer to walk to the reception area myself to greet the client. This conveys to the client that they are important to me and that I want to go out of my way to welcome them and take care of them. Never simply direct or allow the client to wander from the reception area to your office.

Enter the reception area with confidence. Look directly at the client, smile, and say something like, "Hello, I am Mark Chinn. I am glad to see you." Then extend your hand and smile again. A smile makes people feel comfortable. However, be careful not to smile too much or to make light of the client's circumstance. After all, those entering a divorce office have a very serious problem on their hands.

It is very important to look your client directly in the eyes, but not for too long, because a prolonged stare can of course make a person uncomfortable. But a proper look in someone's eyes conveys many things. It says that you are confident in who you are, that you are comfortable and so should they be comfortable. Finally, it indicates that you care about who the client is.

Existing clients should be greeted in a very friendly manner. I usually put my arm around most female and some male clients. This conveys care. It also gives the client the comforting feeling that they are not just a number to you.

The Place of Interview

It is best to conduct conferences in a room other than the lawyer's working office. Our firm has a special client interview room that I patterned after a psychiatrist's office. This is a 12' × 12' room with no window, no desk, no phone, no computer. It is furnished simply with a couch, a coffee table, and a chair for me. I also have a table to the side with hundreds of pictures of my family. The purpose of this interview room design is to facilitate listening. If you interview people at your desk, you will be distracted by the presence of the phone, the computer, and other items in front of you. Your desk is the place where you work and think about problems; it is not the best place for you to listen intently to another person.

If you do not have an interview room, consider using a conference room, which can achieve the feeling that you are taking clients to a special place where all you will be thinking about is them. Make sure, however, that the conference room is not cluttered with boxes or files or other working materials. If you do not have a conference room, consider having a seating area in your office or in front of your desk. Then sit in a chair opposite the client instead of behind your desk.

What to Do First

The first thing you should do is give the client the chance to tell you whatever they want to tell you. Some people may want you to take the lead, but most are busting at the seams to tell you "their story." After the client is seated, say something like, "So, what's the matter?" This question is designed to communicate to the client that you care about their pain. Then they tell their story. Allow the client about twenty minutes to tell you whatever they want to say, whether or not you really need to hear it. This conveys care for the client and respect for what they think and feel.

At times the client may stumble and be unable to tell his story. There are also times when the client may ask you to take the lead. If so, ask simple questions, such as, "What made you decide to come see me today?" or "Did something happen last night to provoke you to call me?" or "Tell me when you got married," or "Tell me about your children." These are simple questions that the client will feel comfortable answering.

Pre-interview Interview

You might want to experiment with using a paralegal or secretary to conduct a pre-interview interview. This would be akin to the nurse in the doctor's office taking a history and blood pressure check from the patient before the doctor enters. This relieves the lawyer from having to take down mundane information such as address, phone, date of marriage, names and ages of children, places of residence over the last five years, employment information, and so on. Another reason to do this is to create a more gradual transition for the client from the outside world to the divorce lawyer's office. If you try this technique, keep the following things in mind:

> The pre-interview person must be pleasant, articulate, knowledgeable, and customer-oriented.
>
> The lawyer should not ask the same questions as the pre-interview person. Doing so conveys a lack of organization and coordination to make the client tell the story twice.
>
> The pre-interview person should not give legal advice, unless she is a lawyer.

Bringing Someone Else

Sometimes the client may bring someone with her such as a trusted friend or a family member. This presents issues of both concern and opportunity. First, the client should be made to feel completely comfortable with the fact that she has brought someone. Assure the client that you are not only okay with this arrangement but that you are glad she brought someone. Greet the person she brought warmly and tell them both you are glad they came, that you thank them for backing their family member or friend in their time of need. Ask your client if she would like to have her friend come to the interview. If she says, "No," ask her if she is sure. If the client elects to bring the friend to the interview, escort them both to the interview room.

In the interview room, assure the client that she made a good decision in bringing support because divorce is a very difficult matter to go through without help. Then, however, you must advise the client that anything said in the interview in the presence of a third party will not be protected by the attorney–client privilege. Each attorney should judge for himself whether to allow a third person to remain in the room. The risk of breaching the attorney–client privilege must be weighed against the advantage of making the client comfortable. One option is to excuse the third party when sensitive matters come up in the client's discussion or when the attorney actually gives advice. In this case, the client should be warned that if she is about to say anything that her companion does not already know, she should stop and give the attorney the opportunity to excuse the companion. To remain absolutely safe with the protection of the attorney–client privilege, the companion should be dismissed before any discussion of the legal matter takes place.

If the client brings children, do not permit them in the interview room with the client. It is a good idea to create a room or space where children can go and relax and enjoy themselves without parental supervision. Stock the room with a television and some children's movies or shows. Coloring books, toys, books, puzzles, and other things should be placed in the room. Paying attention to this detail will show that your firm truly cares about client needs.

Length of the Initial Interview

The length of the interview must vary according to the complexity of the situation and the style of the lawyer. Some lawyers conduct very long and thorough initial interviews, sometimes lasting as long as three hours. The idea is to flush out all possible details in order to make sure the initial advice is founded on all of the facts and does not miss something.

Others hold the initial interview to one hour, for several reasons. First, fatigue sets in after an hour. Second, the role of the lawyer is to give legal advice, not to serve as a friend. Allowing the client to discuss the matter longer than an hour turns the session from a legal interview into a soul-searching chat. I recently broke my rule and conducted a three-hour initial interview. The interview was with a young woman and her overinvolved and emotional mother. The mother dominated the conversation and even refused to leave the room when asked to. I fell into the trap of thinking that if I just took enough time with these people, I could reach them. What happened, however, is that the more time I took with them, the worse it got.

Standard Questionnaire

Standard questionnaires ensure that you obtain the information necessary in the initial interview. These questionnaires can range from fairly limited to extremely detailed. Use a questionnaire that is on the simple and short side. If you get too much information, you cannot digest it. The client is usually not prepared at the initial interview to give the detailed kind of financial information you need. (See Appendix 7C for a Standard Client Intake form.)

Treat Everyone with Courtesy

"People treat customers the same way they are treated."[1] If you yell at your employees they are not likely to turn around and be sweet to your customers. Treat employees as you would a customer and as though you fully understand that they are really *volunteering* to work for you and do not have to be there.

Train your staff to treat everyone with courtesy, whether they are friend or foe, opposing party, or opposing lawyer. This courtesy can take place over the phone, in person, during depositions, and the like, and in all other contacts, such as scheduling depositions or hearings. Nonclients should be treated with the very same courtesy as clients. First, it is hard to be courteous to one person and not another. Second, this treatment of opposing counsel could lead to similar treatment by them, which will make life easier. Finally, this type of treatment may result in referrals in the future from opposing counsel and parties.

Create an Experience

In *The Experience Economy*, Joseph Pine states that "experiences" are a fourth economic offering after commodities, goods, and services. Pine traces the beginnings of a dedication to experience to Walt Disney. He writes that "companies stage an experience whenever they *engage* customers, connecting with them in a personal, memorable way."[2] Consumers encounter "experiences" just about everywhere they go today. Restaurants, movie theaters, theme parks, beauty salons and spas, and even car dealers are selling an experience. In today's economy, no one is interested in buying a commodity; they buy feelings.[3]

The best way to relate to the concept of the "experience economy" is the "experience" you enjoy when you get a haircut. When you walk in, you are always greeted by a very attractive young woman. She usually smiles and says something like, "Good morning, you sure look nice. You don't even look like you need a haircut." After you settle down from the compliment from the pretty young lady, you experience the soft smell of potpourri and the gentle flicker of a candle on a shelf. You sit down and relax. In a corner, a television set is showing beautiful models walking down a runway. You are offered a drink, which is brought to you in a nice glass. Moments later, another pretty young woman ushers you to the place where your hair is to be washed. The hairwash usually takes ten minutes and involves a massage of your neck. You have now been in the salon for over twenty minutes and have enjoyed every minute of it and have still not gotten what you went for: a haircut. But as you can see, the haircut is not why you enjoy going; it is the way you are treated and the experience you have when you get there. Do the people in that salon cut hair better than those at the corner barber? Maybe, maybe not, but you don't care because you get the experience you like at the salon, and you are willing to pay for it.

Lawyers can learn lessons from the beauty salon and other businesses that offer an experience. They must learn the fundamental rule of customer satisfaction: "The competition is anyone the customer compares you with."[4] Therefore, lawyers should do what they can to create an experience that is unsurpassed by any other lawyer. Creating an "experience" is one way to do that.

How does a lawyer create an experience? First, look carefully at the mission statement you crafted for your firm. Take some time and think about the customers you intend to serve. What do they really need? What do they need that they do not even know they need?

Creating an experience in your firm is limited only by your dedication and passion to your clients and your imagination. Look for ways to create your own, unique experience.

Notes

1. Connellan, Tom, *Inside the Magic Kingdom*, p. 96 (Austin, TX: Bard Press, 1997).

2. Pine, Joseph B., III, and James H. Gilmore, *The Experience Economy*, p. 3 (Boston: Harvard Business School Press, 1999).

3. Gerber, Michael E., *The E-Myth Revisited*, p. 155 (New York: Harper-Collins, 1995).

4. Connellan, *Inside the Magic Kingdom*, p. 23.

Dealing with Clients, Part II 13

THE NECESSARY ELEMENTS of proper treatment for the client are education, care, and control. You must educate clients: they must know what has happened to them, what is happening now, and what is going to happen next. They should have a healthy appreciation of the law, their options, the consequences of choices, and each option's likelihood of success.

Clients Must Feel Care

They have hired you for the most important legal problem of their lives. They feel that their entire lives are at stake. They must feel that the lawyer who is working for them cares what happens to them. Finally, the lawyer must have control of the client. The client cannot call the shots. The client cannot remain in prolonged emotional devastation or anger.

Mail

The most fundamental mechanism for properly serving and educating clients is to send them a copy of everything that comes in or goes out of your office. The mailing must be on the day of receipt or delivery by your office. Create a system in your office for insuring that all materials are sent to the client. Train a secretary or other staff person to copy every fax or article of mail and prepare an enclosure letter to the client. Enforce a rule that every piece of office correspondence *must* have "cc: client" at the bottom.

Sending all materials to the client accomplishes many things. First, it is a tangible indication of the work you are performing. This will make your clients confident that you are working for them and will make them feel better about the bill. Second, it keeps your clients current on all developments as they happen. They cannot complain that they were unaware of something happening in their case. Finally, it will educate your clients as to the happenings in their case.

One caveat about sending clients a copy of everything: maintain enough sensitivity to the situation, the client, and the contents of the document to think about whether the client should receive the document in the mail without warning. For example, if the court sends an opinion or order that will be disappointing to the client, delay sending it until the client can be called or counseled in person. The rule in the office should be: "send absolutely everything to the client except when it would be stupid to do so." And remember, if you elect not to send the client a document, record in your file the reason you did not send it or the reason you instructed staff not to send it.

Educational Form Letters

You can enhance client education by sending copies of materials along with very educational letters that explain what the document is, what the law applicable to the situation is, how they should react to the document, and what the next step is. These form letters can be maintained in your case management system and will enable you to "merge" these letters with the client's name and address. Train someone to generate letters for every document received or sent out. Remember: forms are a great source of efficiency, but they must always be examined and, if necessary, customized by a lawyer. Otherwise, errors or embarrassment can result. After a standard set of forms is developed, the firm must continually look for opportunities to develop additional educational form letters to send to clients. (See Appendices 13A–J for examples of educational form letters.)

Educating the Client for Key Events

Clients should be educated well in advance of key events in their case. For example, when clients are told that they will have to attend a deposition, they immediately fear the unknown. As the time for the deposition grows near, they start to wonder if their lawyer is going to prepare them for the deposition or if they are just going to be thrown into the deposition without preparation. There are also critical times in the life of every case when options must be considered or reconsidered and decisions must be made. Clients should be fully educated about these times.

One technique for educating clients at key times is to schedule them in for an appointment. At the appointment, go over their case, mission, and options, as well as the consequences and possibilities of different courses of action and the law. Try to arrive at a verbal understanding of the direction you are going to take and why. Follow the appointment with a lengthy and well-researched "opinion letter" that sets forth in detail the options discussed and the client's choice. Model, form, and opinion letters can be designed to fit the usual situations, allowing for speed of delivery of the product and for efficiency. For example, the choices in any divorce case usually boil down to negotiation between the lawyers or the parties, formal mediation, litigation, or doing nothing. Design a form letter that discusses each of those options. The form should contain basic discussions of the grounds for divorce, elements of alimony, support, custody, and equitable distribution. The form should then be customized for the particular client by inserting the facts of the case and the conclusions reached.

Such a letter has many benefits. First, it serves as a written reminder to the client of the verbal discussions in the office conference or over the phone. Second, it provides the client with a tangible product that will make the payment for time more palatable. And, of course, it serves as legal malpractice protection for the lawyer, since it documents the lawyer's understanding of the facts, disclosure of all the alternatives, and the client's choices and instructions. Legal malpractice protection must always be kept in mind, as many a client will refuse to follow the attorney's advice and then blame the lawyer when the result is bad. Well-crafted opinion letters ameliorate the damage in these situations. Let me give you an example. Years ago, we appeared for trial, but the parties agreed at the courthouse to a divorce on irreconcilable differences and settlement of all matters. The opposing party was an extremely difficult person to deal with who had fought the divorce for no reason. At the judge's instruction, the settlement was dictated into the record and a divorce was entered. Unfortunately, Mississippi law requires that the settlements be *in writing, signed by the parties*. I knew this, and I spent a great deal of time explaining to the client the options she had. She could elect to follow the law exactly, but if she did so, we would not be able to have the written document prepared until another day and we would take the risk of her husband changing his mind and then having to go through everything again. The other alternative was to go with what the judge said to do and hope the matter was never challenged by her husband later down the road. The client chose to get the divorce that day and take her chances.

Well, everything worked out fine for about five years, until the ex-husband hired another lawyer and challenged the legality of the divorce. The former client sent me the ex-husband's motion to set aside the divorce along with a nasty letter insisting I respond for her free of charge and suggesting I contact my malpractice carrier. The passage of five years made me forget the details of the transaction. Although I could not imagine my having approved of a divorce that did not contain a written agreement, I was very concerned—at least until I retrieved her file from storage and saw the ten-page letter I had sent her five years earlier, wherein I confirmed our conversation, her choice, and the law on the subject. I should add that at the time of the deal I believed that we could make the agreement stick, but I was not sure. The law I would rely upon to enforce the agreement was in the letter, and I successfully used that law to defeat the ex-husband's motion. That client never really accepted responsibility for her choice, even after I sent her the letter, but I did get paid and I was able to avoid malpractice or bar complaint. (See Appendices 13K–N for forms to educate clients on events.)

Client Preparation Techniques

Clients should be contacted well in advance of key events in their file and scheduled for preparation counseling. For example, when a client's deposition is scheduled or noticed by the other side, your office should have systems in place to notify the client of the deposition and to give assurance that your firm will prepare them in advance. My experience is that most lawyers simply send the notice of deposition to their clients and pull them aside for a few minutes immediately before the start of the deposition. I know this to be true because I usually have to wait about twenty minutes before I can start a deposition while the opposing counsel and his client meet. Such preparation is unacceptable and leads to extreme client anguish.

Use brochures or videos to educate the client about depositions. Use a Deposition Preparation Checklist so that you cover all essential matters. During the preparation conference, work with the client to determine the client's truthful answers to key questions. The clients' answers can be typed and then given to him to take home and review.

Trial Preparation

The client's education about trial should start in the initial interview and continue all the way to trial. In the initial interview, the client should be told about the alternatives available to him, including the trial. It is hard to say what the client should be told in the initial interview because it depends on the particular case. You should advise the client that taking the matter to trial means that the cost will escalate drastically. Also warn any client desiring a speedy resolution that it takes a long time to get a matter properly prepared and set for trial.

During the course of the representation, the lawyer should have several conferences with the client at key points of the representation where alternatives, including trial, are discussed. Educate the client about the necessary elements of a successful trial and the risks and costs. It is very important that the lawyer not wait until final trial preparation to warn the client that obtaining some key element of relief will be difficult. Personal conferences about the elements of a trial, the risks and costs, should be followed with detailed opinion letters setting forth the client's options, the law and facts, and the consequences of each course of action. These letters will assist both the lawyer and client at that difficult time during final trial preparation when the client looks at the lawyer and says, "I wasn't aware that it would be difficult for me to obtain custody of my children; why didn't you tell me?"

Education of the client should accelerate at the time the matter is set for trial. First, a matter should not be set for trial without careful consultation with the client. Again, the client must be advised of the alternatives, risks, and expenses of trial. And it is very important to consult with the client before agreeing to a trial date—a point of consideration that I believe is lost on most lawyers.

When the matter is set for trial, written notice of the setting must be immediately sent to the client. We instituted this policy several years ago when a very difficult client tried to tell us she did not know a matter was set for trial, just days before the trial. (Of course she did know, but we had no written proof of notification in the file, and this made it difficult to deal with the client.) We now send the client an extensive letter along with the Notice of Trial or Order Setting Trial. (A copy is included in Appendix 13L.) The letter serves as written proof of the notification of the trial date, and also educates the client about what we will do to prepare for trial. Thus, the letter gives the client comfort that systems are in place to prepare them well in advance of trial.

Upon setting the matter for trial, the attorney should immediately calendar dates for advance preparation. We like to have the client in for a preliminary trial prep conference about thirty days in advance of the trial. The purpose of the conference is to confirm necessary witnesses and proof and to draft a preliminary list of questions for the client, opposing party, and key witnesses. Once the preliminary draft is prepared, it is given to the client with a request for review and comment. A conference is then scheduled for the client about seven days from trial and then, finally, a day or two before the trial for final preparation.

Mediation Preparation

Mediation experts state that you should prepare for mediation in much the same way that you would prepare for trial. Of course, you do not subpoena witnesses, prepare witness testimony, or assemble documents for admission into trial. But you should carefully prepare the facts and law of the case and be ready to argue important legal points. The client should also be prepared. Preparation of the client for mediation should begin at the initial interview; at that time the client should be told that mediation is available as a means of resolving her case. You can provide new clients with a brochure explaining mediation. At key intervals in the representation of the client, you should hold conferences to go over the alternatives available to the client. Conferences should be followed by carefully drafted opinion letters that include mediation as an option and confirm the client's instructions in regard to the mediation.

If a client elects to mediate, the instruction to do so should be confirmed in writing. The confirmation letter should be carefully drafted to explain what happens in the mediation process, and to lay out the cost and consequences of going forward with the process. When the mediation is scheduled, the client should be consulted about the date prior to its setting. (A copy of a mediation letter is attached as Appendix 13J.)

In final meetings to prepare the client for mediation, goals for the mediation should be established, and possible courses of negotiation should be charted. Plan at least three "moves." Write down a final, "line in the sand" position. The first position should

be the ideal; the second position should represent a small conces-
sion off of the ideal; and the third should be a position below
which the client will not go. To protect this line in the sand position, have an in-house rule that the mediating lawyer cannot cross
this line without calling in another member of the firm who is not
involved in the mediation. This will prevent a hasty retreat during
the heat of negotiation.

Establishing an ideal and bottom line with the client in
advance of the mediation educates the client about what is realistic. Discussions about the ideal offer will necessarily involve discussions about the facts and the law and the best case scenario in
court. Discussions about a second "move" will help the client see
that he is not going to get his "ideal" position and that it is merely
being developed to provide negotiation room. Developing more
than one position before the mediation equips the client mentally
for the playing of a negotiation "game." It lets the client know in
advance that the other side will reject some demands. Finally,
establishing several moves eliminates delay and waste of time and
money that comes from participants appearing without having
established objectives.

Newsletter

Many organizations utilize newsletters to keep their members
advised about the organization. Newsletters can be equally effective for keeping clients informed. Consider sending a newsletter
with each monthly billing statement. It can inform clients about
the activities and successes of firm members, firm hours, such as
for holidays, and firm procedures. We also provide our clients with
inspirational messages in our newsletter. (See Appendix 130 for a
sample of our one-page newsletter.)

Voice Mail

Voice mail is an excellent medium for maintaining contact between
attorney and client. It allows clients the experience of communi-

cating what is on their mind, even though the attorney is not personally present for the call. In addition, the attorney can leave carefully crafted introductory notes on the voice mail which inform the client of where the attorney is and when the attorney is likely to get back to them. For example, a voice mail message might say, "I will be in deposition out of town for the next two days and back in the office on Thursday when I should be able to return your call. If you have an emergency, please press zero for my assistant who knows how to reach me in such cases." The importance of this message is that the caller is forewarned that the lawyer cannot get back to them until Thursday.

Calling the Client with Important News

Attorneys should remember that clients are usually on "pins and needles" about developments in their case and that one of the attorney's most important obligations is to relieve that natural tension whenever possible. For example, an attorney who enters a divorce for a client should call the client from the courthouse or from the car on the way back to the office after obtaining the divorce. I will never forget an incident about fifteen years ago. I had entered a divorce for a lady on December 29 and then promptly put the signed papers in the mail to her. I thought I had done her a favor by working on a day when most people do not and promptly obtaining her divorce at the earliest opportunity. But when I talked to her on January 2, she blessed me out: "You ruined my New Year's holiday by letting me believe I was still married!" She was really mad, and all of the positive feeling from the excellent work I had done for her over the previous months was lost, all because I did not call her when I got the divorce.

Clients need prompt notification about any development. Often lawyers do not call clients after simple motion hearings or pretrial conferences, believing the results are not earth-shattering. But to clients, any development in court or on their case is earth shattering. To put this matter in better perspective, think of yourself as having had a biopsy for cancer and you are awaiting the results. What is it like waiting and wondering if you have cancer?

Well, it is bad. How would you feel if the doctor did not call you when he knew? You would feel that he had deprived you of a happy life for those days you waited unnecessarily and you would feel as though he did not care about you. Well, waiting for a legal result is much the same to our clients; it is like waiting to find out if they have cancer. We must be sensitive to this and respond as promptly as possible to alleviate their anxiety.

Touching Base

One element of service that is often ignored is the random status check. Many lawyers may become skilled at calling the client at critical times but may neglect calling the client at random just to see how they are. The attorney will have to judge whether to charge for such a call, but it should go something like this, "Hello, Mrs. Jones, this is your lawyer. Don't be concerned, nothing bad has happened in your case. I am just calling to see how you are."

Personal Interviews at Critical Times

There are times during the representation of a client when you can just tell that the client is struggling, or does not understand something, or has lost sight of the big picture. When that happens, do not let the client hang out there in uncertainty. Schedule a conference so that you can go over the case together. Such interviews should be followed with a letter confirming the discussions and the direction to be taken.

Personal Touches

Look for ways to bring a personal touch to your representation. Clients should feel that you *know* they are in the legal fight of their life, that you *know* they feel their entire lives are threatened, and that you are going to take *personal care* of them. Below are some of the techniques you may use to show a personal touch.

A Personal Card

Send a personal card. When a client mails you a check, send a personal card saying thank you for the check. Have a staff member send your clients a personal note that says the lawyers are thinking about them. Send a card upon the birthday of a child or the death of a family member.

Free Call after Hours or on Saturday or Sunday

Calling clients after hours or on weekends builds trust. Simply take a name or two home and make the calls after hours. It will take twenty minutes out of your evening, but will tell the client you care enough about them to call after hours. Another way to achieve this effect is to visit the office for a couple of hours on Saturday and make a few customer service calls. The impact is tremendous. Here is how such a call might go: "Hello, Mrs. Jones, this is your lawyer, how are you?" Mrs. Jones, "I'm fine, but what are you doing working on my case on Saturday?" Lawyer: "Well, I was just up here taking a look at your file and making sure things were going as planned, and I just thought I would give you a call at no charge to make sure you are okay and to let you know I care about you."

Clients will tell you that Sundays and holidays are tough on them emotionally. So, one technique for communicating care is to make a small list of clients to call on a Sunday or a holiday. It can take anywhere from fifteen minutes to an hour, but the dividends are enormous in the client care department. A conversation might go like this: "Hello, Mrs. Jones, this is your lawyer, how are you?" Mrs. Jones, "I'm fine, but what are you doing calling me on Thanksgiving?" Lawyer: "Well, past clients have told me that holidays can be tough, so I just thought I would call you to let you know that I am thinking about you and I am behind you in this difficult time."

Calls or Letters at Sensitive Times

Just as it is important to call the client for major events, such as hearings, and holidays and Sundays, it is also important to give the client a call during sensitive times. For example, you represent a young mother who has just separated and is concerned about allowing her small child to go away for visitation. Give this client a call when the visitation is to take place to let her know you support her. Or a mother is sending her child away for extended summer visitation for the first time. A phone call or card to let her know you care about her will be much appreciated. Other sensitive times might be the day a client tells his spouse he wants to separate, or the day one confronts a spouse about alcohol use.

The Value of the Hug

I started practicing law in the late 1970s. It seems that during the late 1970s and early 1980s, everyone was extremely sensitive about sexual abuse claims, and it was verboten for a professional to show physical affection for employees, coworkers, or clients. Maybe that is the way it still is, I don't know, but I have always believed in showing physical affection for people. For many years I have made it a habit of putting my arm around clients or hugging them. In the early years, I wondered if that was appropriate, even though it felt right to me. And then, one day, a deeply religious woman whom I had represented in the past told me that she missed "those old bear hugs [I] used to give her" when I represented her. I thought to myself, "if this woman views the hug as a sincere expression of care, then I am going to keep doing it." I have done it ever since and without incident.

Coaching the Client to Turn Adversity into Opportunity

Domestic cases are full of adversity from start to finish. Any experienced trial lawyer will tell you that things never go exactly as planned. The key is to not let the difficult times get you down. The same is true for the client. It is just as important to manage client emotions as it is to manage client legal problems. The reason is that if your client gives up because of emotion, the case can be lost when it should not be lost. Develop the habit and skill of coaching your clients to embrace adversity and to view every apparently negative circumstance as an opportunity. For example, just the other day I was meeting with a client who had just read his spouse's deposition. He was beside himself and kept saying, "She is lying, she is lying. How can she lie? You have to do something about her lying." He was so angry, he was giving me a headache, until I thought to say, "Hey, be *glad* she is lying. That means we are going to have plenty of ammo for trial. You should be concerned if she was telling the *truth* and there was nothing we could do at trial with it." He seemed to understand that.

Creating Boundaries

Providing excellent and caring service does not mean that attorneys should put up with mean, abusive, or inappropriate conduct. Examples of such conduct by difficult clients are as follows:

Excessive cursing

Failing to pay or "not receiving the statement" or asking for an "itemized statement" after they have been sent many

Prolonged anger or grief

Prolonged or excessive desire to "get" the other person or cause them pain

Cursing or abusing staff

Telling the lawyer he must do something exactly the way the client instructs them

Refusal or inability to follow advice

Every person involved in a divorce is entitled to some anger and resentment, and they might even be entitled to brief abuse of the lawyer. But the lawyer must tolerate only a little of such conduct. For example, if a client curses and hangs up on a secretary or paralegal, this is a sign that the client has needs or issues that cannot be adequately addressed by the law firm. When such conduct takes place, the lawyer should talk to the client and say something like, "I understand you are having a difficult time with your divorce and we are here to serve you, but we need to have some ground rules for our working relationship. One of those rules is that you cannot abuse or curse me or the staff. That interferes with our ability to help you. Can I have your assurance that it won't happen again?" The healthy client will reply, "I know, I am so sorry. I just couldn't take it when you told me about all the lies he told in his deposition. It won't happen again."

Anger or grief in a divorcing individual is normal. If there are no signs of anger or grief, you probably have a problem on your hands. But it is also normal for anger or grief to diminish over time. When a person does not get over his anger or grief and keeps subjecting you to it, he probably needs to find another attorney. For example, I have often said that you should create a service orientation in your office which treats people as though they have just emerged from surgery. I developed this theory after a recent surgery of my own. I was hospitalized for four days after hip replacement surgery. I was on morphine for most of the time, and I was not a happy camper. I recall cursing the nurses in the middle of the night and throwing a water bottle across the room, among other things. Now, if someone on the hospital staff had yelled at me, I would never in my life have forgiven them. I was in great discomfort. But if I had continued to act in that way after the initial recovery period, it would have been wrong. By that time, it is normal to be healed. Reprimand for bad conduct after the normal recovery period would then be appropriate. The same is true for our clients. It is normal to be in pain about the divorce but unhealthy to stay in pain. The attorney must establish boundaries on the expression of this pain in order to represent the client properly.

The attorney must also establish boundaries on payment for services. Many attorneys delude themselves into thinking that they are doing the client a service when they represent them without demanding payment. Most attorneys are "people helpers," and many enter law practice with a spirit of service to humanity. Because of that attitude, they are often lured into the unhealthy conduct of serving people without demanding payment. They think this sacrifice on their part will build intense client loyalty. But the opposite is true. The only thing that working for free builds is a lack of respect by the client. If you think about it, how can the client believe you will fight *for them*, if you are a pushover *with them*?

When a client has not paid his or her bill in thirty days, she clearly does not intend to pay. You must then talk to the client. The conversation should go something like this: "You have not paid your bill. Do you have some questions about it or are you unhappy with some level of our service?" Client: "Well, I don't have any money right now and I don't want to ask my family for help. I couldn't do that." Attorney: "Well, if there is ever a time to ask your family for help, it is now. I am your attorney, and it is important that our relationship remain as an attorney–client relationship and not become a debtor–creditor relationship. That is not in your best interests, and I will not continue on that basis."

There are a few clients who want to tell you what to do. This type of client will demand that you do something and then will blame you when things do not go the way they expected. This is true even if you warn them and get them to sign a disclaimer. I have had clients who sent me a letter or pleading demanding that I send opposing counsel the document they had prepared without change. Then, when I sent the document and it produced an extreme retaliatory action on the part of the opposing party or counsel, the clients called me and scolded me for not carefully reviewing the document. In their mind, it was my fault. Maybe it was, but not for doing what they said; rather, it was for continuing to represent clients who thought they could control my actions. If you think about it, those clients had little respect for me as an attorney to believe they could treat me like that. Thus, when a client seeks to dictate your actions in extreme fasion, get out of the representation if you can.

If you cannot get out of the representation, do what you think is right, not what the client demands. Some months ago I was trying a custody case for a lady, and at a critical point in the trial, she insisted that I cross examine a witness about the opposing parties' practice of listening to a certain kind of music. She insisted that I introduce a tape of the music into evidence. She was certain this was critical evidence. Well, to my mind, it was silly and would detract from an otherwise strong case. I will never forget the conversation with the client in the courtroom: Client: "Okay, put the tape in now." Chinn: "No." Client: "I am the client and you must do what I say or I will report you to the bar." Chinn: "I am not putting the tape in; it won't help. As a matter of fact, it will hurt." Client: "I'm telling you, Mark, you better put the tape in." Chinn: "No." I didn't put the tape in.

Exit Interview

It is important to finish your service with a ceremony and remind the client of the excellent job you have done. Simply stated, people may not fully appreciate what a fine job you have done for them if you do not tell them. One way to accomplish both ends is to conduct an exit interview after all of the work is completed. We like to hold it at about the same time the divorce is granted, if not the same day. The exit interview has four basic parts. In the first part I revisit everything that has happened, obstacles cleared, difficulties conquered, wins in court, and so on. I usually open up the file and start at the beginning, "Well, I see we opened your file last August 17. You were concerned that you did not have grounds for divorce and that your husband would challenge your custody of your children because of your alcohol use. We went right to work and got an alcohol evaluation, which proved negative, and then we filed suit and set the matter for a temporary hearing. We got custody of your children and then moved quickly to settlement talks. We ended up with an agreement and a divorce within four months. Not bad." It is positive to go back over the difficulties and how they were overcome and to implant in the client's mind the value of your work. This is good for you *and for your clients*. They need to feel they did well in hiring you.

Clients also need to feel good about themselves. Frequently, I will conclude the first part of the exit interview by saying, "You know, I want to tell you something: I am proud of you. You handled a very difficult situation, and you never let anger get the best of you. You never retaliated against your husband's dirty tricks. You handled your divorce with class." Or, "I know you didn't want a divorce, and I know you are probably feeling like a fool for trying so hard to save your marriage, all to no avail. But I want to tell you that you should never second guess yourself for doing everything you could to save your marriage. I am proud of you."

The second part of the interview is a discussion of the elements of the agreement or order. Go through the agreement and talk about the various provisions, discussing what they mean. Discuss what the settlement talks were and how you tried to get a more beneficial provision but just could not get the other side to go for it. Discuss how you might have advised the client that a certain part of the agreement was not a good idea, but they elected to do it anyway. For example, "I advised you that you did not have to pay this much alimony, but you elected to do it anyway, saying that you wanted to make sure the mother of your children had enough to live on. You didn't have to do that, but I salute you for that; things may work out best for you in the future because of your generosity." This type of discussion cements the give-and-take of the negotiation in the client's mind and gives a realistic remembrance of how things went. This will help both client and lawyer in the future if things do not go right.

The third part of the exit interview is the "advice and warnings" section in which the client is advised as to how the order may be enforced or modified, what to do and not to do, when to come back for advice, and how to protect himself. (A copy of the exit interview checklist is included in Appendix 13P.)

The final part of the exit interview is the *celebration and farewell*.[1] I got this idea from a real estate agent who sent my mother a bouquet of flowers when she moved into the home she had helped her buy. I thought, "I must do the same for my clients." So, we give our clients a bottle of champagne at the end of the exit interview. I might say something like, "I know nobody wants to divorce, but we must view all adversity in our lives as an opportunity. Take this champagne as a token of our affection and gratitude and get together with your closest friends tonight and pop the cork and say a toast to your new life." For some clients, we expand the idea. One particular client went through pure hell with his case, with his business partner and wife double-teaming him with conspiracy and litigation. He paid three times what he should have had to pay for his divorce because of the conspiracy. But he never complained and gave us all the resources to do a good job for him. After his exit interview, we threw a surprise party for him, inviting several of his close friends. Recently, we concluded a long and expensive battle for an oil man who likes to smoke cigars. Again, this client went through hell, but he never took his pain out on us. We presented him with two bottles of fine champagne and a set of fine Cuban cigars. We called all of the staff in and popped the cork on one bottle of champagne and had a brief firm party with him. I was advised just the other day that one of my associates saw this former client in the grocery store, and he said, "I miss seeing y'all. Can I come by to see you?" And then he jokingly added, "You won't charge me, will you?"

Divorce Entry Checklist

When the divorce is concluded, often many details remain to be taken care of, such as the transfer of property, preparation of QDRO's, the closing of accounts, arrangements for insurance, and the transfer of automobiles. Great service to the client involves monitoring these details and assisting the client in tying up loose ends. The best job of closing a divorce file I have ever seen took place at the office of an opposing counsel several years ago. We were at his office and signed the papers. At the same time his secretary presented the agreement and order of divorce, she also brought out a series of documents and forms: a bill of sale for the boat that was being transferred, a tax form for the wife to sign allowing the husband to claim the children as dependents, a quit claim deed for the home, and a QDRO for the pensions. There were no loose ends! She had it all taken care of right then and there.

Many times it is not possible to close all of the details at the time the agreement is signed. For example, the parties might agree to transfer property after the divorce, or a payment of money is scheduled six months down the road. The service-oriented attorney develops a checklist for these matters and follows up for the client. (Attached as Appendix 13Q is such a checklist.)

Service after the Sale

Most lawyers view the entry of the divorce as the *end* of the case. It may be the end of this case, but excellent opportunities for service present themselves in the post-divorce period. You might call this "service after the sale." Service after the sale helps distinguish your firm's service from others, it helps clients avoid pitfalls, and it provides excellent, continuing marketing opportunities with past clients.

When our firm closes a file, we create calendar reminders for key dates in the future. Some examples are as follows:

Thirty days—Call the client thirty days after the file is closed just to see how she is doing. This is similar to a nurse calling a patient several days after a surgery just to see how the patient is feeling.

Five-month checkup—Most rules of procedure require challenges to any judgment to be raised no later than six months following the entry of the judgment. Contact the client at the five-month point just to check on them and advise them that if they have any valid reason—such as fraud—for challenging the judgment, they need to let you know.

Annual—Clients should review their judgment or agreement at least annually. (A standard "anniversary letter" is included in Appendix 13R.)

Key payment dates—If a client has to make certain payments, calendar the dates of the payments and send a friendly reminder. This helps clients avoid contempt and lets them know you are thinking about them. It also keeps your name in front of the client for the purpose of referrals. Calendar the dates on which payments decrease or terminate, such as the date children reach majority or the date the last alimony payment is to be made.

You probably cannot charge for the service after the sale work. Consequently, you must make these contacts more efficient and less time consuming by creating forms that can be generated by nonbilling staff.

Note

1. Herman, Gregg, *101+ Practical Solutions for the Family Lawyer*, p. 539 (Chicago: American Bar Association, Family Law Division, 2003).

Trial Preparation and Presentation 14

YOUR TRIAL PREPARATION SHOULD BEGIN from the moment your client walks into your office. Your advice to the client in the first interview should be given with trial in mind, even if you never intend to go to trial. If you do not plan for the ultimate possibility of trial, you will not give good advice and you will be one step behind your adversary. You will also compromise your ability to negotiate because you will not be functioning from a position of power.

During the initial interview, briefly question the client to determine whether the facts of the case fit within the legal definitions of the legal options available to the client. For example, you should ask if the client has the ability to prove the various grounds for divorce, such as adultery, drunkenness, and cruelty. If separation has or may occur, question the client on whether he would take his spouse back in order to see if a separate maintenance action can be maintained. Question the client on the criteria the court will use to determine custody. Question the client on the ownership and acquisition of property to see how the proof stacks up for trial.

Questioning the client about the facts they can ultimately prove at trial helps you not only to assess risks, provide options, and chart a course, but also to advise the client on what gaps in proof need to be filled. For example, the client tells you her husband is a drunk, but upon questioning, you find that she has no way of proving it. Therefore, in the initial interview you immediately instruct the client in the acquisition of evidence, such as collection receipts or charge card documentation of liquor purchases, taking pictures of the spouse passed out on the couch, and talking to friends for testimony about drunkenness.

Get the Research Right Away

Even experienced lawyers neglect to research the law as it might apply to each case, even at the point of trial. Never forget that the foundation of all of your efforts is precedent or statute. Obtain pertinent research at the very beginning of the case, so that your case planning will be on solid ground from the outset.

Deposition

Depositions must be taken with a clear understanding of the elements needed to prove important aspects of the case. Depositions should be taken with the intent of providing a foundation for cross examination at trial. (Logically, you only take depositions of adverse witnesses.)

Before taking a deposition, develop a "mission" for the deposition. Know why you are taking it and what you hope to accomplish. For example, you are about to take the deposition of the opposing man in a custody battle. Your mission might be: "To find out what proof he might have which would be a problem for us and to establish that he cannot meet the criteria of a primary care giver." One set of questions would simply be designed to find out what his "best shot" at your client might be: "What evidence do you have that (my client) is not a good mother?" The second set of questions is designed to pin him down and provide possible fodder for cross examination.

What are the names of your child's teachers?

What is your daughter's dress size?

What subjects is your daughter studying?

It's true, isn't it, that you didn't plan your daughter's birthday party?

It's true, isn't it, that you didn't play tooth fairy?

Lay these "attack questions" out in the fashion and order you would like to use them at trial. If the answers are the ones you want, you will have your trial questions all done. Then, when you prepare for trial, lay the deposition out in front of you and type the same questions from the deposition, noting on your question sheet the page and line of the answer. This allows for easy retrieval for impeachment.

Here is another example of knowing the law before the deposition. A lawyer recently took the deposition of a psychiatrist for the purpose of trial testimony to support a claim of habitual cruel and inhuman treatment. The lawyer asked all kinds of questions about the treatment, the condition of the patient (her client), and what the prognosis was. However, the lawyer never asked the direct question required to obtain a divorce on cruelty, that is, "Did the treatment constitute a danger to the health of (the client)?" or "Was it impossible for (the client) to remain in the marriage?" These questions incorporate the legal standard of the finding the judge has to make to grant a divorce on the grounds of cruelty. The judge denied the divorce. The moral of the story is that you should research the elements you have to prove before the deposition and then incorporate the *exact language* of the legal standard in the questions. Do not beat around the bush.

Another example involves a lawyer who wants to prove adultery and starts asking questions: "Did you date? Did you kiss? Did you see each other? Did you exchange cards?" Baloney. The first question for a lawyer seeking to prove adultery should be: "Have you had sexual intercourse with someone other than your husband during your marriage to your husband?" Then, if you want to ask other questions, fine. Again, make sure your questions go to the heart of the matter and use the *exact language* from the case or statute that supports your position.

In my view, it is malpractice not to take the deposition or statement of every likely witness against your client. You should never ask a question in trial when you do not know exactly what the witness is going to say. I am sure you have heard the old story of the trial of a man in England for biting another man's ear off. The defense attorney was questioning the prosecution witness and got the witness to admit he had never seen the defendant actually bite the ear. Smelling blood and pressing forward, defense counsel then asked a question whose answer he did not know: "If you didn't see him bite him, then how do you know he did?" The answer: "Well, I saw him spit the ear out."

If taking the deposition of every likely opposing witness is not possible, consider interviews. You might say, "they will never agree to talk." Well, they might if you use this line: "I understand you may not want to talk with me, but I am really trying to do you a favor by interviewing you. You see, if you don't talk to me now, over the phone, I have the right to issue a subpoena to you to have you come to my office during your work hours, at a time convenient to me, to ask you any relevant question, under oath, in front of a court reporter. The choice on how convenient you want to make this for yourself is yours." Trial planning should always involve planning far enough ahead to obtain the identity of such witnesses and to arrange for their deposition or statement. Once you have a list of witnesses, go over it with your client and seek his input on whether or not depositions need to be taken. Carefully determine with your client which of the opposing witnesses may be most likely to testify. Then ask your client if he has some idea about what they might say. Obtain the client's assistance in determining whether the deposition must be taken. Cost is going to be a factor for most clients, so this process is important.

Calendaring

Calendaring is critical to effective trial preparation. Computerized calendars allow you to set appointments for yourself or to give yourself reminders. Failure to use a *system* for reminding you to start preparations may result in failure. You should carefully consider what systems you can use to make sure nothing slips through the cracks. Under our system, when a matter is set for trial, we immediately calendar it on our case management system. We have programmed our case management system to provide us with reminders at key intervals going backward from the trial setting. For example: sixty days, thirty days, fifteen days (last days to issue subpoenas *duces tecum*) prior to trial, and so on.

The Sixty-Day Meeting

At sixty days from the trial date, conduct a preliminary trial preparation meeting. Get your support staff together and go over the status of the case. What is the status of discovery? What are the witnesses we might use? What documents will we use? Have we properly supplemented discovery? Do we have all the evidence we need? Do we need to subpoena any documents or order any appraisals? Do depositions need to be taken? Develop a checklist of matters that you wish to cover at the sixty-day trial preparation conference. (A Trial Preparation Checklist is contained in Appendix 14A.)

The Thirty-Day Meeting

The same questions should be asked at the thirty-day meeting as at the sixty-day meeting. The answers and timing of things are of course, a little more urgent. Many things that *might* be done at sixty days *must* be done at thirty days. For example, failure to supplement discovery with an important witness at sixty days might be okay, but failure to do it at thirty days might result in loss of the witness for failure to timely supplement.

At the thirty-day meeting, start the preparation of the trial notebook—the manuscript for the trial. It contains the lists of witnesses and documents, questions for each witness, key research, and so on. Something about physically setting up the notebook and using it as a foundation for preparation enhances the trial preparation. Set it up and base all of your subsequent preparation on filling in the blanks in the notebook. For example, begin by completing a list of witnesses and documents. Then, structure your subsequent preparations to complete the questions for each witness listed.

The Fifteen-Day Meeting

Fifteen days prior to trial is a critical date for effectively completing any pretrial tasks. It is the "drop dead" date to plan and issue subpoenas *duces tecum* (most rules of procedure requiring ten days' service for subpoenas *duces tecum*). Deciding to issue subpoenas for trial later than fifteen days can result in problems. The witnesses you need may be on vacation if you try to serve them the week before trial. A key witness for your client might be out of town on a business trip if you wait too long to talk to him about coming to trial. Fifteen days is also an appropriate time frame to call the client and arrange a preliminary trial preparation conference.

Trial Preparation Meetings with the Client

You should meet with your client at least several days in advance of the trial. During this meeting, a rough draft of questions for the client and a cross examination of opposing witnesses should be developed. I usually have the client sit opposite my desk as I turn to my computer to type questions. I involve the client in preparing the questions. Sometimes, the client is involved very little and simply sits there as I go through my plans for the questions. Other times, the client is closely involved in structuring the questions. For example, I recently represented a major in the army. He appeared at his trial preparation conference with a disk containing all of the questions on it. As it turned out, the questions were excellent, and I made very few changes.

I usually go over the client's answers to each question and type the answers into my list of questions. I might use italics or bold print to distinguish the answers from the questions. At the conclusion of the interview, I print the questions and answers for the client and other witnesses and give them to the client, asking for a review of them and determining whether we need to add or change anything. We then schedule a final trial preparation conference on the afternoon before trial.

Clients grow very nervous as their trial date appears. When the matter is finally set for trial, they start wondering what the trial is going to be like and whether or not their lawyers are going to prepare them properly. Therefore, you can ease a considerable amount of anxiety if you advise your client early of what you are going to do to prepare for trial and how and when you will involve them. Do this verbally and with the use of a standard letter. (A copy of such a letter is contained in Appendix 13L.)

Document Preparation

One of the things that really slows a trial down and distracts the judge from the flow of the message is the admission of documents. Efforts should be made to arrive at agreements with opposing counsel prior to trial as to the admission and numbering of documents. Our firm attempts to hold pretrial meetings with opposing counsel to exchange document lists and to prenumber documents. Most opposing attorneys are too poorly prepared for this to work, but when it does work, it speeds up trials greatly. Whether or not we have cooperation from opposing counsel, we like to prenumber our documents. We usually supply opposing counsel with our trial documents, whether or not they ask for them. That way we eliminate any possibility that they will be excluded for some discovery issue. Of course, the voluntary supply of documents is a trial strategy decision that must be carefully considered, as there may be legitimate *surprise* considerations.

As you script your testimony for each witness, put a notation in the script for the document you intend to use. Next, carefully order your witnesses. Then, go back through your script and create a list of documents in the order in which they appear in your script. A well-trained staff member can do this for you. Then have the documents numbered in the order in which they will be used at trial.

Always have four copies of each document at trial: one for you (and perhaps included in your trial notebook), a second for introduction into evidence, another for the judge, and the last for opposing counsel. We like to prepare an exhibit notebook for the judge so that the judge has all of the documents in front of him. When questioning a witness, you can refer back and forth to documents and simply tell the court, "this is found under tab 6 of your notebook." Judges love this convenience. They have their own set of documents to look at as they hear the testimony, and they can make notes on them. Prepare an identical notebook for opposing counsel. Opposing counsel may object to the notebook for the judge for any number of reasons, but I can assure you, the judge views such a notebook as an excellent tool. In one of the best trials I ever participated in, both counsels agreed to prepare a joint financial statement and a joint exhibit notebook for the judge. Hundreds of exhibits were quickly admitted into evidence, and the judge was provided her own notebook for easy reference. Notation was made of the objections each party had to documents, and those objections were handled in orderly fashion with little delay. The judge was effusive in her praise of both sets of lawyers in her opinion, because the lawyers had made her job easier.

Time Blocking

Many lawyers go crazy with panic prior to trial. About a week before trial, they start to work very long hours and on weekends. They frequently work very late on the eve of trial. This causes considerable friction with the staff, because the lawyer becomes demanding and short tempered and requires the staff to work after hours.

Proper planning and use of time will eliminate panic-driven preparation and late hours on the eve of trial. Use of calendar reminders and the preliminary trial preparation meetings at key intervals are excellent tools to eliminate panic-driven preparation. Another tool is *time blocking*. Well in advance of trial, figure out all of the things you need to do to get ready for trial. Then, make appointments for yourself on your calendar to do those things. For example, if you conclude you should interview four witnesses, pick out two or three times on your calendar and make an appointment for yourself: "interview witnesses." Or you need to organize and number your documents, so you schedule four hours four days before trial. Another example, you know you need to set aside basic preparation time, so you calendar an afternoon appointment for yourself five days before trial: "trial preparation."

Responding to Discovery

Failure to handle discovery properly can result in trial preparation disasters. Discovery to your client must be answered properly and timely. Discovery responses from your client must be sufficient to help you prepare for trial. You must manage your firm to create systems to make sure discovery is handled properly.

When you receive discovery requests, send the client a letter with the discovery advising the client of the nature of the discovery and warning the client that failure to answer the discovery properly and honestly could result in making key evidence for the client inadmissible. Use calendaring reminders to make sure you have supplemented answers in a timely fashion prior to trial. At the trial preparation meetings, the witness and document lists must be compared to the witnesses and documents listed in responses to discovery. (A discovery checklist for this purpose is attached as Appendix 14B.)

Calendaring and reminder systems should be used to prompt you to check on receipt of discovery answers from the opposing party. The moment discovery is propounded, a staff person should calendar the date the discovery is due and follow up. Discovery answers of the adverse party should be checked at the sixty- and thirty-day trial preparation meetings.

The Notebook Method

Good lawyering is precise business. It requires neatness, and it should be handled the way you would want your surgeon to handle surgery on your brain. I cannot tell you how many lawyers I have seen come to trial with folders of loose, unorganized papers and several legal pads with scribble on them. They eschew neatness, saying they like their sloppiness because it is what they are comfortable with and they know where everything is. Baloney. I usually end up handing these lawyers documents they cannot find and helping them pick up the loose papers that slide out of their folders.

Precise trial preparation and presentation is best accomplished with the trial notebook—a three-ring notebook where you place everything critical to trial presentation. Our trial notebook contains the following:

Facts. Create a one-page statement of the facts. Include names of the parties, names and ages of the children, incomes of the parties, a basic list of assets, and other key facts or dates. When you present an argument to the judge, you can quickly flip to this section to make sure you have the accurate facts as you speak. For example, most judges like to see the attorneys in chambers to find out what the case is about and see if matters can be settled or simplified. I usually open my notebook to the facts section and start: "Judge, this is a thirteen-year marriage, the parties have three children who attend public school, the wife is a homemaker, and the husband is a surgeon earning $850,000 per year, the parties have the following assets." And for a nice touch, I hand the judge and counsel opposite a copy of the fact sheet for a visual reference as I speak.

Pretrial Matters. This section is designed to remind you of the matters that need to be resolved before trial—for example, motions in limine, special arrangements for testimony of a witness, evidentiary issues, introduction of an expert report, use of an appraisal instead of a witness. As trial preparation proceeds, make notes in the notebook of matters you do not want to forget to bring up to the court before the trial begins.

Witnesses. In this section, list the witnesses for each party, preferably in the order they might be called. For your witnesses, list their phone numbers so you can call them when you need them; for opposing witnesses, include a brief statement of what the discovery says they will say. If documents are not too voluminous, put copies of them in the notebook in the section for the witness for which they are to be used. Put the condensed copies of depositions of witnesses in the section for the witness. Highlight important parts of documents and depositions so that you can easily find the pertinent part. Proper use of the notebook and inclusion of copies and documents allow the lawyer to access everything easily without leaving the podium. It looks very smooth.

Documents. List the documents you intend to use in the order you will use them. When you make such a list, you are better able to assess your preparation—that is, do I have the document? Can I get it? Will there be questions as to its admissibility? In addition, the list should be compared to your answers to discovery to make sure you have properly identified the document in discovery, so you can use it.

Witness Questions. Create a divider for each witness at trial. Use the notebook to spur you to proper and thorough preparation of questions for each witness. As you approach trial, make sure you have specific questions for each witness in your notebook. Don't go to trial with an empty divider for a witness. Remember, first-rate preparation requires a deposition or interview for each witness and a thorough scripting of questions *to which you already know the answer.*

Research. Put in memorandums of research or cases relevant to the issues.

A properly prepared trial notebook is all you need at trial. You can carry the notebook home with you during the evenings of multiday trials, or during breaks and at lunch. You need nothing else. Everything is tabbed, labeled, and at your finger tips. Use nothing else.

Getting to Court 15

CREATE A CHECKLIST OF ITEMS that you might want to have in court. One or two days before court, fill out the checklist and give it to a staff member with instructions to pack your trial brief cases for you and have them ready at a certain time. (Appendix 15A contains a Brief Case Packing Checklist.)

Amend your checklist as you learn what you need. For example, a female associate said the checklist should contain an extra pair of panty hose in case there is an unexpected run. You might think that is silly until you get caught in court, several hours from home, with an embarrassing run in your stocking. Our checklist also includes food and water. We usually pack cheese and crackers, pretzels, and the like. Just the other day I was in an emergency custody hearing and we worked through lunch. Our expert was on the stand through lunch. At a break, she looked at me and said she felt her blood sugar was low. I said, "Would you like something to eat? We should have something over here." She said, "Yes." When I looked in my brief case, there were the cheese and crackers.

Prepare a Case Brief

For trial, you can seize the advantage by preparing a brief and proposed findings of fact and conclusions of law and submitting them to the court in advance of trial. Preparing these documents assures you that you have properly researched your case and planned the development of your proof. It also serves as a reference for the court in making its decision and rendering its opinion, and it puts the other side off balance if they have not done a similar product. Recently, I tried a case and submitted a brief and proposed findings to the judge and opposing counsel on the morning before the trial. The opposing counsel had not planned to do this, but seeing my product, he did not want to be outdone, so he stayed up all night working on it and presented his product to me the next morning. He may have evened the score, but he tried the case with a whole lot less sleep than I did.

You may be thinking, "Wait a minute, you said in Chapter 5 don't prepare a brief." You are right, but the point is that you should *first* present the *single-case method* and supplement it with a brief. The court cannot miss the single case, but it may not read the brief.

Arrive Early

The prepared person arrives early, at least twenty minutes before any hearing or trial. More importantly, the lawyer should always arrive ahead of the client, so that the client will not have to experience the natural anxiety of wondering whether the lawyer is going to appear. Clients should be escorted and guided, not left to fend for themselves. Always tell your clients—who are almost always thirty minutes late—to arrive about thirty minutes before you really need them.

Get the "Lay of the Land"

When you arrive at court, walk around, talk to court personnel, get comfortable with the people. In other words, get the "lay of the land." Walk around the courtroom and get comfortable in it. Pick the seat you want. If your client arrives early enough, let her sit in the witness box to see how it feels.

Be Courteous

Always treat opposing counsel like a brother or sister in the practice of law. Greet them with a friendly hello and a handshake. Break the tension with them with small talk or light humor. Treat opposing parties and witnesses with courtesy and without any personal affect at all. Be polite and nonjudgmental. Remember, court is for the *civil* resolution of *civil disputes*. Intimidation, unfriendliness, lack of courtesy have no place in court and bring disrepute to our system of justice. You should explain to your client before you go to court (or depositions or other hearings) that you will be courteous to opposing counsel and parties and witnesses. If you do not give an advance warning, your client may misinterpret your conduct as disloyalty. In addition, instruct your client to treat opposing counsel and party and witnesses with courtesy and respect. Tell her to greet her spouse properly in court. If your client can handle it, instruct her to approach opposing counsel at the appropriate time and introduce herself and shake hands in a friendly manner.

Provide Documents to Opposing Counsel

Treat opposing counsel with complete forthrightness prior to trial and show everything you intend to introduce into evidence. Of course, if you have been able to follow the trial preparation plan, discussed earlier, you have already pre-marked all documents and have secured opposing counsel's objections or agreement to every document. But if you have not done that, show opposing counsel your evidence and ask for his. This will expedite trial and will also relieve some of your tension. You will also find that when you attempt to introduce evidence, the judge will often ask, "Has opposing counsel seen this?" It shows your professionalism when you are able to say, "Yes, your honor."

Sharing evidence with opposing counsel can create an opportunity for settlement. The other day, I attended an emergency hearing with a young lawyer whom I did not know. Since it was an emergency hearing, there had been no discovery. I felt I had the upper hand in the matter because I had superior facts, preparation, and witnesses. The opposing party was a young mother in need of treatment. If we tried the case, we might "win" custody, but we might also fail to get the children's mother the treatment she needed. So I sat down with opposing counsel and offered to share what evidence I had. She thanked me and took all of my materials and met with her client. Within a short time, we had worked out an agreement for her client to go into in-patient therapy for two months while my client took care of the children. My client's objectives were achieved: custody of his children and treatment for their mother.

Image in Court

An essential part of any presentation is appearance, including that of the lawyers, the client, and the witnesses. Every element of appearance must be consistent with neatness and preparation, down to whether your shoes are shined.

Carefully pick your attire for court depending on who you have to communicate with. Of course, you must always be yourself, but you can vary your attire for the audience with which you must communicate. For example, if I am going to appear before a Judge who is also a member of the National Guard, I might wear grey pants, blue blazer, white button-down shirt, and a red, white, and blue tie. If I am appearing in front of a judge who attended a particular school, I might wear that school's colors. If I am appearing before a stylish judge, I might wear a vivid color, such as a bright green tie. But whatever a lawyer wears, it should be neat and dignified, bringing honor to the judicial process.

Always appear in court with your documents and other materials neatly organized. All materials should be in labeled folders and boxed in new boxes, neatly labeled with the contents of the box.

Clients and witnesses should be instructed in how to dress

and conduct themselves. (See Appendices 15B and C). I learned this lesson many years ago when I appeared in city court to defend a client on a charge of indecent exposure. I was very worried because my client was a respectable businessman and there was no apparent way to make sure the judge would believe him instead of his accuser. That is, until his accuser showed up in court. She was a tall woman wearing an extremely short, tight-fitting, leopard skin skirt, with red high heels and a low-cut blouse. I turned to my client and said, "I believe we just won the case."

Buddy System

There is an old joke about the client sitting next to his lawyer in court. The other party was represented by two lawyers. The client asked the lawyer how come the opposing party had two lawyers. The lawyer replied: "When one lawyer is up talking, the other is thinking." The client thought for a moment and queried, "When you are up talking, who's thinking?"

Court is tough. The lawyer's attention in court is drawn in many directions, from client service to paying attention to opposing counsel, to managing file materials, to managing witnesses, and to adapting to the judge. It is of great assistance to take a "buddy" with you to court. Preferably, the buddy should be another lawyer or a well-trained paralegal. But, if you do not have that luxury, at least take your secretary.

Communicating to the Court

Your law office should have systems, procedures, and training that are designed to systematically aid you in presenting your case. Here are some techniques and systems.

The Communication Triangle

I have learned that effective communication consists of a single main message, surrounded by three explanatory or supportive concepts. The idea is to weave the language of the main message and supporting concepts into everything that is said. This communication concept can be visualized in the form of a triangle.

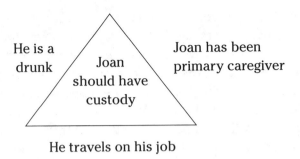

He travels on his job

The communications triangle can be used in preparation for arguments or testimony and it can be used for both lawyers and clients. When preparing clients, prepare a communications triangle and give it to them to take home.

Illustrations for the Court

Before making any presentation to a judge, prepare simple exhibits that illustrate your case. One such exhibit is a fact sheet. When introducing your case to the court, hand the judge a fact sheet, which contains basic facts such as names and ages of the parties, length of marriage, names and ages of the children, incomes of the parties, and perhaps assets. Remember, the judge has to assimilate a lot of information fast, so a simple fact sheet will help.

Another such exhibit might be an asset list that features the contentions of each party. This asset list will have columns to represent the various claims of the parties as to values and classification of property. This exhibit can bring all of the pertinent financial issues before the court in one single page. (Such an exhibit is illustrated in Appendix 15D.)

Another such exhibit might be an income comparison and child support calculation sheet showing the incomes and budgets of both parties and a statutory compilation of support. It might also show how much income each party will have after payment of support in relation to their budgets. This will help the judge visualize the pertinent issues in regard to support.

Use your imagination. You should always look to create a one-page visual of the key issues that support your case. Such visuals should be part of your preparation system.

The "What We Want Sheet"

The "What We Want Sheet" states your demands for the court. I have prepared meticulously for court many times and then realized at the end of the testimony that my client's desires had never been clearly formulated, much less presented. The "What We Want Sheet" prevents that. It should be built into your systems, so that you never go to court without it. You can hand this sheet to the judge at the beginning of trail, in the opening statement, during your client's testimony, or during closing argument. I will never forget the first time I realized the magic of this sheet. I handed the judge this sheet with all of the pertinent issues on one page. The judge held my sheet before him during the testimony and made notes on it, and I realized that he was evaluating all testimony in light of what I had demanded. When he rendered his bench opinion following the trial, he read from notes made on my "What We Want Sheet." (See Appendix 15E for a sample "What We Want Sheet.")

Document Notebook

Give the judge a tabbed, indexed notebook of all the exhibits; this will allow the judge to review exhibits as you present evidence, to make notes on the exhibits, and to flip back and forth among the exhibits as the testimony is presented. Finally, it gives the judge a tool for formulating the decision.

Have a Prepared Order

Before you go to court on any matter, prepare an order that grants the relief you want. If you want to go a step further, prepare one or more alternative orders. There are many reasons to do so. First, preparing such an order helps you clarify what you are trying to accomplish and therefore helps you structure your presentation to achieve your goals. This tip comes from that great Illinois trial lawyer, Abraham Lincoln, who advised, "Always prepare your decree before you go to court." Second, being able to say, "Your honor, I have taken the liberty of preparing an order," displays not only preparation ability but confidence. Finally, having an order ready for signature prevents delay and avoids the possibility of drafting conflict. Our firm always goes to court with a proposed order or agreement and a laptop and printer to make changes if necessary.

Case Management 16

FOR YEARS I LIVED IN FEAR, waking up in the middle of the night, worried that something terrible was about to happen the next day, that perhaps I had forgotten some important deadline. On a few occasions, I actually threw my blue jeans on and drove to the office at 3:00 in the morning. Of course, when I got there, I quickly realized there was no emergency. To help you sleep well at night and to avoid malpractice suits, effective, reliable case management systems must be employed.

The Calendar

Many firms use a large calendar on which they manually record key trial dates and deadlines. Such a calendar is obsolete in the age of case management software and should not be relied upon as a method of case management. However, even if case management software is used, a large calendar can be useful as a visual aid to view key dates in the future.

Docket Sheet

A docket sheet is a list of each case with a summary of key information. It lists the case and the lawyer responsible, and gives a brief summary of the status of the case and any key dates in the future. The docket sheet assists each lawyer and staff member in keeping track of the status of cases. The docket sheet also serves as a reference for discussion during docket meetings. (An example of a docket sheet page is contained in Appendix 16A.)

Docket Meetings

Most lawyers and firms are so busy that they fail to stop and assess what they are working on and what needs to be done. Often, lawyers fall into the trap of working on what they want to work on, instead of what needs to be worked on, and cases get neglected. Regular docket meetings help make sure that cases do not fall through the cracks. The docket meeting is also a time when the entire staff can take a few minutes to think about a case and brainstorm about what steps should be taken.

Our firm has a one-hour docket meeting every Monday morning from 10:30 to 11:30. The entire staff participates, from receptionist to bookkeeper to attorneys. Usually, we talk about each case for at least a few minutes. We try not to leave discussion of a case without setting a date for when something is going to happen or some action is going to be taken. Setting out a date for action or for review keeps the firm's performance proactive instead of reactive. Staff records these dates in the case management system.

Docket meetings are also a time to talk about many things other than the management of the case. The bookkeeper is present to talk about the status of the account: "Is there a retainer in trust?" "Is the account past due?" "Is the client cooperating in payment?" If not, the firm must take steps to protect its financial integrity. This type of discussion keeps the firm from working and working and building up a huge (and probably uncollectible) past due account without noticing it.

Firm problems can be discussed in docket meetings. Perhaps there is a problem with equipment that should be discussed. Perhaps there is a quirk in the filing system.

Docket meetings can also be used for morale purposes. At these meetings, inspirational writings can be read and discussed, and awards can be given. Docket meetings can be fun, too; meetings that are not fun may be counterproductive.

The docket meeting should be on everyone's calendar; the purpose of the meeting can be defeated if everyone is not in attendance. Our firm conducts the meetings on Monday mornings before we get going in the week. We schedule no hearings, depositions, or appointments at that time.

Everyone must participate. A few years ago, I had an associate who would bring file materials and read them during the meeting. Everyone in the meeting recognized that this person regarded the docket meeting as a waste of her time.

Docket meetings (and case management) are most effective when the entire team understands the questions that need to be asked. A couple of years ago, I realized that every meeting consisted of me asking the members of the team all of the questions. It got to the point where the meeting seemed more about members answering my questions properly instead of managing the cases. People felt they were being graded. This hurt morale. As a solution, I devised a sheet of the questions I typically ask about cases, and I handed it out to the team. When we had meetings, I asked different team members to ask the pertinent questions from the sheet. The purpose was to systematically train the entire staff—no matter how much experience they might have—to ask the same questions I might ask. Over time, the question sheet disappeared, and the entire staff began to participate. Most often, the answers to the questions are now conveyed before the questions are asked. This fosters a feeling of confidence among the members of the team. (Attached as Appendix 16B is the docket meeting checklist.)

In addition to regular docket meetings, meetings of key people should be conducted to discuss files at critical intervals. For example, in the docket meeting it becomes evident that a case is stalled and nothing is happening. To resolve that problem in a docket meeting would take too much of the entire staff's time and unnecessarily lengthen the docket meeting. So this is a time to schedule a case management meeting of the key lawyers and staff people involved in the case. Perhaps an hour can be blocked out on the calendar to conduct such a meeting. If your firm consists of just you and the secretary, get the secretary to meet with you. Whether your firm is composed of many lawyers or just one lawyer and a secretary, the meeting creates a time to focus on the case and to put minds together.

Case Management Software

If you are reading this book and you do not have case management software, put the book down immediately and acquire some. You should not operate another day without it. Among other things, case management software allows you to create reminders in the computerized calendar. These reminders can be manually created. If you desire to check on a client in thirty days, you go into the system and create a reminder in the client file for the desired date. Most systems allow you to create a reminder after taking notes on a phone call. You open a window for the phone call, type some notes, and then click a button in the phone call window to create a reminder in the future. For example, you are talking to a lawyer about preparing an order. The lawyer says she will prepare the order and get it to you in a few days. The case management system allows you to create a reminder to check on the matter in a few days, just to make sure the other lawyer does what she said. Finally, case management systems allow you to program the calendar so that it will systematically and automatically remind you of dates. For example, you can create a simple program to give you reminders in advance of the scheduling of a matter for trial, such as sixty-day, thirty-day, and fifteen-day reminders prior to trial.

Time Management 17

MOST LAWYERS WHO READ THIS BOOK probably go into work every morning and just start working, not wanting to delay getting things accomplished. They move from matter to matter, or phone call to phone call, or to a fax or letter as it comes in, working on what hits them, when it hits them. Such days are busy and hectic—but usually chaotic and not as productive as they can be. Such a day usually ends up in failure to accomplish priorities. People who manage their time in such a manner are the people who do not call you back.

To Do List

To increase efficiency, create a "to do list" for the day. There are many different forms of such lists, the most basic of which is a simple listing of the things you want to accomplish. The list can be improved by listing things to do in the order you wish to accomplish them. The most effective list I have seen is a simple A, B, C list. Draw three lines horizontally across the page. The first section is the A section. This section contains matters you *must* accomplish that day. Do not put anything in the A section unless you absolutely must do it today. Putting too many matters in this section sets one up for failure because it is impossible to accomplish too many absolutely critical tasks in one day. The B section is made up of matters you would *like* to accomplish today but do not *have to* accomplish today. And, finally, the C list contains matters you need to accomplish this week or those that you do not wish to forget. (See Appendix 17A for an Attorney's Daily Worksheet.)

Morning Time

Successful people put a lot of effort into starting the day early and in proper fashion. They wake up early, work out, observe some quiet time, eat a healthy breakfast, and then carefully plan their day. No one would expect a pilot to take off on a flight before carefully preparing his flight plan or a builder to begin building a house without a set of plans. Neither should a lawyer begin his daily work without carefully planning exactly what he is going to do *before* commencing work. To increase efficiency, take fifteen minutes before you start the day and carefully prepare a to do list.

Quiet the Mind

An offshoot of taking morning time is taking time to "quiet the mind." Studies tell us that good performers learn to quiet their brains during successful performance.[1] Meditation is an excellent way to quiet the mind. Deep breathing exercises can accomplish quieting the mind in a short time. Daily, morning planning helps to quiet the mind by ordering thoughts and priorities.

Put Files Away

Have you ever seen a lawyer who has his files stacked all over his office? These lawyers keep their files in their office because they feel that keeping the file in front of them will remind them to work on it. However, such a practice leads to inefficiency and error. The first problem it presents is the danger of file materials from one file becoming commingled in another . . . and thus being *lost!* The second danger is that clients will see other client materials. This is unprofessional, and it also makes the client wonder if you are letting other people see their file. Finally, keeping a file in the office makes it difficult for other people to find the file when they need it, especially clerical staff who need to file materials or another lawyer in the office who has to answer a client question. Instead of keeping files in your office to remind you to work on them, put the matter on your "to do" list and put the file away.

Be Disciplined

Follow your plan for the day and do not allow yourself to get sidetracked. For example, you might have planned to work on drafting a complaint from 9:00 to 10:00 one morning, and then you receive a fax. Your first inclination is to read the fax, the "late-breaking news." Of course, once you read it, you have a tendency to start thinking about how you should respond to it. You then stop working on the complaint and start crafting your response to the fax. But then a call comes in from a client. Your client has a problem and wants you to write a letter to opposing counsel, so you stop working on the response to the fax and start working on the letter to opposing counsel. An hour has now passed and the complaint you wanted to work on is not done, the response to the fax is not done, and the letter to opposing counsel is not done, because one of your staff members just walked in with a question you need to answer.

When you make a plan, follow it; do not allow distractions. If a matter arises, make note of it on your to do list and deal with it later. Have your staff block calls to you during certain work times. Or if you are working on something and a call comes in, tell the secretary to take a message.

Create Routines

Successful performance comes from routine. Any golfer will tell you that the "pre-shot routine" must be the same every time.

Watch any bowler and see that she approaches picking up the ball, taking her stance, and delivering the ball in the same way every time. Watch any tennis player and you will see that every serve is delivered after the exact same routine. Watch any basketball player shoot a free throw. They will bounce the ball the same amount of times, breathe, twirl the ball the same way every time before shooting. Lawyers should do the same.

Here is an example. Wake up at 5:45 every morning, walk the dog, go to the gym, cook breakfast, shower, and arrive at the office at 8:00. Review the calendar for the day, check e-mails, listen to phone messages, and then take fifteen minutes to plan the day. Read mail from 8:30 until 9:00; make phone calls from 9:00 to 10:00; take appointments from 10:00 to 12:00; go to lunch; return calls from 1:00 to 1:30. You get the idea. The key is to study your habits, likes, and dislikes, and times when you are most efficient and then create a routine that you follow every day. Do it exactly the same way, every day, just like Michael Jordan shoots his free throws. Whenever possible, do not allow judges, opposing counsel, or clients to disturb your routines.

Task Blocking

Just as a car is built more efficiently with the use of an assembly line, so can you increase your productivity by performing certain tasks at certain times. For example, phone calls are usually pretty short, but each phone call is an extreme interruption that requires the lawyer to quickly assimilate his thinking to the matter at hand. To become more efficient, schedule the making and receiving of phone calls for certain times. Block out time in your workday for receiving, making, and returning calls. For example, I find that I am a little tired right after lunch. Phone calls are relatively easy for me to handle at that time. So, I block out from 1:00 to 2:00 most afternoons to make and receive calls. I have my list of calls to make, and I just start dialing. I might be able to make about ten calls in an hour. As a result, the calls are marked off my "to do" list, and I might have billed two and half hours in an hour (10 times .25).

Research is difficult because it requires extreme concentration. Interruptions by either phone calls or staff totally disrupt research. Therefore, block out time on the calendar for the research, just as if you had an appointment with a client. Allow no interruptions, focus totally on the research.

Time Cop

If you have problems with disciplining yourself, enlist the aid of a "time cop." I learned this technique from the practice management folks at Atticus, in Orlando, Florida. Atticus provides coaching and mentoring for lawyers. They suggest you enlist the help of a paralegal, secretary, or other key aide to make you follow your own rules. This person makes sure you create a plan and follow it; perhaps screens your calls and interruptions by staff: and checks with you during the day to make sure you are billing time and sticking with your plan. All of us need accountability, and the time cop provides it.

Monitor Yourself

At different times during the day, stop and ask yourself, "How am I doing?" For example, stop your work at about 10:00 in the morning and ask, "How many hours have I billed?" Or "Am I sticking with my plan or allowing myself to get distracted?" If you are doing poorly with your billing, stop and think about how you can "catch up." If you need to catch up, you might change your task list to group many tasks that take a short amount of time, require little thought, and create a standard billing entry. For example, you reach lunch time and see that you only have an hour and a half of time billed. You need to catch up. So review your to do list, and group several short phone calls and letters together. These tasks are not difficult, do not take much time, and can generate a quarter of an hour time entry per task. You might realize at mid-day that you have worked hard but have not accomplished the key task you needed to accomplish that day. Stop what you are doing, refocus and return to your priority task, and get it done before you do anything else.

Eliminate "Fish Files"

"Fish files" exist in most lawyers' offices. They are the files that sit in the far corner and start to stink because they have not been worked on in many months. The lawyer does not want to work on them for some reason, but keeps them in the office to remind him to work on them. Fish files interfere with productivity because they act as a constant drain on the lawyer's conscience and psyche. If you have some fish files, list them on your to do sheet as *must do* items and get them done. Stop the stink!

Create an Ending Time

It is a universal law of time management that the task expands to the time allotted. Therefore, allowing more time than is necessary for the performance of a task is inefficient. (Most lawyers allow an unlimited time to perform their work during the day.) The lawyer works many hours and brags to friends about how long he worked, but the truth is, he probably could have gotten the same amount of work done in two-thirds the time, if he had been efficient. A corollary of the universal law that the task expands to the time allotted is that performance improves to meet a deadline. Combining the universal law and its corollary means that you should create an "ending time" for your day. You should set your ending time at the *beginning of the day*. The limit on your work hours should hang out there like a deadline to force you to finish your work. Maximum efficiency is obtained when this ending time is a *routine*. Know every day, as a matter of routine, when you are leaving work.

Do not fall into the trap of thinking that many, many hours of sacrificial work is the object; it is not. The object is to perform legal tasks well and to bill the amount of income necessary to accomplish your goals. Do not worry if you are the last one to leave; worry how good your work is and whether you are meeting your objectives. Those who work all hours of the night are probably not efficient. They may simply be trying to impress themselves or someone else. Or they have nothing better to do.

Scheduling Rules

Use scheduling rules to enhance your efficiency. Study your tendencies, strengths and weaknesses, and experiences and create rules that meet your objectives. During my work with my Atticus coach, Shawn McNalis, several years ago, I developed a set of scheduling rules that I will share with you. These rules came from a careful analysis of what stressed me, what created inefficiency, and what made me feel productive. Here they are:

Nothing on Monday

I do not allow any scheduling on Monday. Monday is the day to assess the week and plan. It is a day to retool after the weekend. Monday follows two days of being off of work. Monday morning should be absolutely sacrosanct as a time to evaluate cases and determine the work to be performed during the week. I might allow a client appointment to be scheduled on Monday afternoon as an exception, but that is it.

Just think, if a trial, deposition, or hearing is scheduled on Monday, what is the first thing that happens? You got it. You work on the weekend. That is bad enough, but even worse is that you are working on Sunday and you realize you need something for the Monday hearing that you cannot get on a Sunday. Then what will you do? You might need a secretary to type something, but she is not there because it is Sunday.

A few years ago, I was at the club swimming pool talking to one of my lawyer friends. In the middle of the conversation, he sadly put down his beer and started collecting his things to leave and stated, "Well, I hate it, but I *have* to leave. I *have* to catch a plane this afternoon for Miami." He said this like somebody was making him do it, but I did not believe him. I cross examined, "Well, who's in charge of your schedule?" He smiled, knowing that I had nailed him, and said, "I guess I am." I said, "Well why don't you schedule that deposition for Tuesday, or are you just trying to pick up some extra, easy billed flight time on Sunday? Me, I'd rather spend it with my family." He said, "You're right." But I bet he is still scheduling Monday depositions in Miami.

Nothing Before 9:30

Like Monday, the first part of the morning is critical for analyzing and planning and getting accustomed to the workday. The first part of the morning is for quiet time and planning. Then, phone messages, e-mail, and mail must be reviewed, and priorities for the day must be assessed. Appointments before 9:30 interfere with that process and create havoc for the day.

No Back-to-Back Appointments

In working with my Atticus coach, Shawn, I learned that having to go from one appointment to another without delay created unnecessary stress for me. Though exciting, back-to-back appointments exhausted me and also hurt my performance. I learned that while I was in the second appointment, I was still thinking about the first one and having trouble remembering the facts pertaining to the second. I decided that I needed a "buffer" time in between appointments to decompress from the first appointment and to review the file for the second so that I would be fully ready for the second client before she came in. This buffer time not only reduces my stress, but makes me a better lawyer for the second appointment because I am better prepared.

No Appointments at 1:00

Bad things happen when appointments are scheduled at 1:00. First, the client might show up early, that is, before 1:00, when no one is back from lunch and the door is locked. This leaves the client standing outside the office, wondering if you remembered the appointment. Second, the client might come in at 1:00, but you are not back from lunch yet. This leaves the client in the waiting area waiting on you, which is bad. Third, you may return to the office and see the client in the waiting area and feel obliged to begin the appointment without organizing yourself and properly preparing for the client.

No Back-to-Back Day Scheduling

Before scheduling a hearing or an appointment, check the day before and the day after. For example, I do not want to schedule a client appointment or deposition on the day before a trial. The day before trial should be reserved for trial preparation and focus. Similarly, matters such as depositions and hearings should not be scheduled the day after significant depositions or hearings because there will have been no time to prepare. Certainly, you can do it, but it will create stress in your life, diminish your preparedness, and ultimately, shorten your life.

No Lunch Appointments

Often, a client will say that he wants to see you at lunch. Your standard reply should be, "No, I eat lunch at lunch." You must be healthy to perform well, and not eating lunch is not healthy.

No Early Out of Town Hearings

I try to ask court administrators to see if I can schedule hearings out of town at times other than 9:00, such as 10:30. Sometimes the judge will not permit it. But if you say something like, "Will you see if the judge will let me have the hearing at 10:30 so I can get up at a reasonable time to get there?" sometimes they will. You should do this to avoid upsetting your routine. Remember the value of the routine. Your routine is broken by getting up at 4:30 instead of 5:45, and showering and driving without working out and eating breakfast and seeing your kids before they go off to school. If you have to drive an hour and a half to another town, a 10:30 setting will allow you to stick to your routine.

No Friday Afternoon Appointments

Friday afternoon is probably the worst time of the week to get work out of either yourself or your staff. For most, Friday afternoon is just not a serious time.

Respect Holidays

Whenever possible, do not schedule hearings or depositions right before or right after holidays. For example, in December, do not schedule hearings on December 23, when your staff and court staff and other people want to be off. I recently allowed such a scheduling on an emergency motion and found myself unable to subpoena key witnesses because their businesses closed on December 20. As my hearing proceeded into the afternoon of December 23, I found myself without key staff members who had previously arranged for vacation time during that day. If you schedule a hearing immediately after the holiday, you ruin the holiday for yourself, your staff, and perhaps your client as well. You also risk not being able to access what you need in the two or three days prior to trial because businesses and court and law offices are closed during those days.

Time Off

Modern thinking on efficiency is more and more turning toward the value of rest. In the epic book *The Power of Full Engagement*, Jim Loehr and Tony Schwartz concluded that the key difference between the very best tennis players and ordinary players was the capacity of the best to *rest* between points.[2] The same is true, they state, for all other professions. Lawyers are so used to the concept of working long hours that they regard "rest" as a dirty word. Recently, I was sharing a cocktail with one of my best lawyer friends on New Year's Day. As he opened a beer in my kitchen, this very fine lawyer with thirty years of experience bragged to me how he had worked until 6:00 P.M. on New Year's Eve! I told him, "You know, I am more interested at this point in my career in seeing how little I can work." My point is that everyone should schedule times to rest.

Additional Resources

For additional information on managing time, see, "95 Tips for Effectively Managing Time" in Larry Holman, *11 Lessons in Self Leadership* (Lexington, KY: Wyncom, 1995), pp. 105–111.

Notes

1. Murphy, Shane, *The Achievement Zone*, p. 144 (New York: Berkley Books, 1996).

2. Loehr Jim, and Tony Schwartz, *The Power of Full Engagement* (New York: Free Press, 2003).

Financial Management

18

ONE OF THE MORE IMPORTANT DECISIONS you will make is your bank. Ideally, you should select a bank that is very close to your office. This will make it easier to make deposits, pick up cash, and visit with your banker. In addition, you should select a bank where you can have a personal relationship with people who handle your account. There are going to be times when you will need advice, times when you will need overdraft protection, times when you will need the immediate assistance of a banker. Pick a bank where you know you will have great personal service.

Another consideration in picking a bank is business. When interviewing bankers, ask if there is any opportunity for you to receive some bank business. When I was in the early years of my practice, my bank allowed me to do foreclosure and collection work. This was a huge help to my bottom line.

Setting Up Accounts

You should set up three accounts:

1. *Operating Account*—for depositing fees and paying out expenses.

197

2. *Trust Account*—for depositing client retainers and
    other trust funds.
3. *Salary/Tax Account*—for paying out taxes and salary
    and making payroll deductions.

More Than One Person Handling Funds

Good cash management principles require that the person who
receives money should be different from the person who deposits
money. This ensures a record of receipts that is independent of
the record of deposits. Ideally too, the person who handles
deposits should be different from the person who records payment on client accounts, but few small firms can have three separate people involved in the process. The person who receives the
checks should record the checks received each day. This record
can then be compared to deposits and client accounts to ensure
the integrity of the process and to deter employee theft. Talk to
your CPA about designing a plan that fits your office.

Create Rules for Receipt of Funds

Rules for the receipt of funds depend on your staff. If you have a
small office and wish to have absolute control of the money, make
it a rule that only you may receive client funds. Whatever you do,
make sure each employee knows what he or she is supposed to do
when money comes in.

Cash Receipts

Never allow the receipt of cash by your firm without providing the
payer with a receipt and maintaining a copy of the receipt. Office
supply stores sell a book of receipts that allow you to give a
receipt and maintain a copy. Get one of those books and keep it in
an appropriate place, such as the front desk or the bookkeeper's
desk. *Never accept cash in excess of $10,000.* The IRS may cause

you trouble if you do. Never accept several payments in a case from a single client which amount to more than $10,000. The IRS is smarter than that.

There will be times when a client will offer to give you cash so that you do not have to report it. Say "Thanks, but I will be reporting all funds received." Make sure you tell your client that, and make sure you give him a receipt. Someone who is friendly today may turn you in later.

Trust Account Considerations

The number one ethical consideration in terms of finances is to make sure that client funds are never commingled with the attorney's funds. Even an honest mistake can result in suspension by the bar. Therefore, before setting up accounts, consult your ethical rules. You might also personally consult with your bar's complaint counsel or law practice management personnel before setting up your accounts. When you receive funds from a client, you must decide whether the funds are to be deposited in your operating or your trust account. For example, if a retainer check of $5,000 is received, do not deposit that check in your operating account where it will be commingled with your operating funds. Such a mistake, though innocent, could result in ethical problems for you. If you receive a check for payment on the account which exceeds the amount owed, deposit the entire check in trust and then write a check from trust to your operating account, leaving the unearned balance in trust. Of course, if you receive a check for the amount owed, or less than the amount owed, you may place the entire amount in operating.

Never, never, never take money from client funds (trust account) without *written* permission. This rule applies in every circumstance and no matter how good a relationship you have with the client. This is a rule of business and ethics which must always be followed. The first place you can record written permission is the contract. Your contract should grant you specific permission to remove client funds from trust for payment of your bills and for payment of expenses incurred in the client's representation, such as deposition and filing costs. If you receive funds for the client, such as a check from the opposing party to pay attorney's fees, treat the funds as client funds. Place them in trust and then obtain written permission to pay your fees with them.

Credit Cards

Credit cards are an excellent vehicle for receiving payment. Contact your bank to see about setting up a credit card account. There are two downsides to credit cards, however. First, there is a percentage fee for their use, such as 3 or 4 percent, though I regard this as a small price to pay for facilitating payment. The second problem is that clients can reverse credit card authority without warning and contest charges.

Setting Aside Taxes

One place that lawyers get into trouble is failing to set aside money for taxes, either for themselves or for payroll. The bills for these taxes can be big and unexpected. And the IRS and the Department of Labor do not have a sense of humor about such things.

As an employer, you are responsible for withholding taxes from your employee's wages *and* withholding extra money as employer contributions. To assist you in setting aside these funds, determine what amount of withholding you will owe over and above the gross salary of the employee. Then pay that amount plus the gross amount due the employee from your operating account into your salary/tax account. Write the employee's check for net wages out of the salary/tax account. Retain the extra money in your salary/tax account for payment of the withholding and payroll taxes when they are due.

Income tax estimates come due every three months. If you are doing well, your estimated payments every three months are going to be big amounts. If you have not set aside money for these payments, you are going to get caught owing a huge amount with nowhere to get it. It is very important to budget a monthly payment from your operating account into your salary/tax account to accumulate the taxes you will need for your quarterly estimate.

Hidden Taxes

Talk with your CPA about taxes that you might owe over and above income and payroll taxes. These taxes include local personal property taxes and unemployment taxes. Believe it or not, your city and county government may tax you for the value of the personal property you have in your office. They will ask you to estimate the value of this property on a yearly basis, and they will visit your office from time to time to audit your estimate. Budget for this and other less well-known taxes.

Bookkeeping

The management of money lies at the heart of the success of any business. It comes before anything else, even the delivery of the legal product. If you do not make and keep money, you will be closing shop and getting a job with someone who does pay attention to money. The first thing you need to do when you open your own business is to manage your money as if you were an institution.

Hire a CPA

One of your first acts when you start your own business must be to hire a competent CPA. Ask his advice on what records you should keep to properly manage your business.

Use the Computer

Your checkbook should be computerized to allow for accounting and reporting through the use of computer software. Many programs are available that are both inexpensive and easy to use.

Generate Monthly Reports

Whether you can generate the reports in house, or you need an accountant to do it for you, you should generate monthly general ledger, balance sheet, and income statements. You must look at these critical financial management documents at least once a month.

Dashboard

In addition to the standard financial documents (balance sheet, income statement, and general ledger), you should create a custom report that gives you the key financial information you need to manage your business. The people at Atticus call this critical sheet a "dashboard." They liken this report to the dashboard of your car, which is designed to instantaneously give you the critical information you need. Again, the dashboard should be customized to provide the information that *you* think is important. My dashboard contains the following:

- Hours billed by each staff member, versus their salary, with percentage of billing to salary
- Total hours billed for the firm
- Amount of money received as a result of time billed by each staff member versus their salary, with percentage of billing to salary
- Total receipts for the firm for the month
- Number of files opened this month, last month, and last year at this time
- Accounts receivable this month, last month, and last year at this time

(A sample dashboard is presented in Appendix 18A.)

Cash Flow Reports

A cash flow report tells you how much money you have and how much you might need. This information helps you plan and determine how much effort should be put into collecting accounts receivable. (A sample cash flow report is shown in Appendix 18B.)

Budgeting

Budgeting is a function that any business must perform. A budget includes the income you think you can generate minus the expenses you will likely incur.

Income can be determined by first calculating the number of hours you think you and your staff can reasonably bill. For example, a standard work month is 160 hours (40 hours per week for four weeks). A standard work year is 2,000 hours. Determine if you can bill more or less than these standards; then multiply that number by the hourly rate for each producing member. This will give you a projected income. Reduce that number by a projected percentage of uncollectible accounts.

Determine your expenses. If you have a history of expenses from years past, plug these past expenses into your budget and then go back and examine each expense to determine whether the amount should be increased or decreased in the coming year. For example, you might determine to cut your expenses next year. Upon examining your meals budget, you see that you spent quite a bit on meals for yourself and associates and referred sources. You determine that the value of the lunches did not justify the expense, so you elect to eat at home next year and cut your meals budget by 80 percent. You also examine your book budget from last year and see that you spent a lot of money on books but did not use them. You therefore elect to cut the book budget next year. You also want to increase your income. You see that you did not spend a lot on business promotion, and so you elect to increase the business promotion expense in hopes of increasing income.

Treat Your Business Like a Business

Many people reading this book will likely be small firm or solo practitioners who are in total control of the money in their business. When you have total control, the tendency is to lose structure and accountability. There is also a tendency to use your law office accounts as though they were personal. For example, you start making purchases of groceries or home items out of the office operating account. Such practices are dangerous for several reasons. First, when you do not discipline yourself to use your business accounts for business matters, you lose the ability to carefully monitor the success of your business. In short, you cannot tell how your business is really doing. The financial records are skewed or clouded by the personal expenditure. This, in turn, makes it difficult to make decisions or alterations that are necessary for financial success. Second, you lose track of your spending and can easily start living at an inflated level, which will ultimately lead to excessive debt. Finally, business books that are muddied with personal expenses do not exemplify the kind of financial integrity that lenders or the income tax agencies like to see.

Positive Aspects of Debt

Debt can help you achieve many objectives long before you would otherwise. The best example is your home purchase. If you had to wait until you had the funds to purchase a home, you might never save enough money. In addition, we all know that the interest can be deducted from a home loan and homes are usually a good investment. So debt can be positive. In your business, debt can help you purchase or lease a computer system. Debt can help you purchase an office building. Debt incurred to obtain the necessary tools of your trade can be positive. Whenever you incur such debt, calculate how you will be able to pay it back. For example, if you are currently billing $200 per hour and you need a new computer system, you might increase your hourly rate to cover the additional monthly expense.

Negative Aspects of Debt

Do not incur any debt that is not carefully calculated to lead to income or that you have not carefully budgeted for. Be very careful of utilizing lines of credit for anything more than emergencies. Once you run up debt, you develop a monthly interest charge. The debt grows, and you suddenly have another budget item on your monthly budget. It is hard to pay it back.

The Line of Credit

Talk to your banker about establishing a line of credit. You always have a line of credit in place to make up for temporary cash shortfalls. Be very careful about the use of lines of credit, however, for they can lead to an unhealthy sense of wealth, which leads to spending beyond your means.

Form of Business

Consult with a local business lawyer about your form of business. I recommend that you start or create your business in the form of a professional limited liability company or a sub chapter S corporation, or similar entity in your jurisdiction. The reason is liability protection. Of course, it will be difficult to escape personal liability when you are a solo or small firm professional, but you should employ every means available to protect yourself. You should also consult with your CPA for income tax considerations.

Insurance

Give careful consideration to the many different kinds of insurance you should have. Find one insurance agent whom you trust and tell him that you want to know all of the different kinds of insurance that you might need and what they might cost. See what types of insurance you can afford. The following are the types of insurance you should consider:

Malpractice—You must have malpractice insurance. Practicing without it is foolhardy, and perhaps impermissible in your jurisdiction. One way to find the different coverages and prices available is to consult with your local bar, which may have a list of approved companies. You can hold the cost of this insurance down in different ways. One way is to obtain a high deductible. Another is to find out what types of work might drive your premium up and then choose not to do that type of work.

Business Liability—As a business owner dealing with the public, you are open to suit for matters that are not malpractice. Do not fail to obtain general business and premises liability.

Umbrella—As a lawyer, you will serve on boards and be involved in the community. You will also be sued by angry opponents for things like malicious prosecution or abuse of process. See if your agent can provide you with protection from all possible exposures through umbrella coverage.

Auto Insurance—Talk to your agent about making sure you are insured for liability from acts of employees such as auto accidents. Do not rely on your employee's auto insurance to cover you.

Fidelity Bond—If you have someone in your office who handles money, obtain insurance against theft by purchasing a fidelity bond.

Business Interruption—This insurance will protect you if you become disabled. It will pay some expenses of your office to keep it running in the event of your disability.

Disability—Most law practice management consultants and financial advisers will advise you to obtain disability insurance.

Getting Better 19

CREATE A MINDSET that says, "I am going to get better every day. I am going to look, observe, notice, analyze, and think every day about how I can create systems to make me better." Your ability to continually improve is essential to your success. Success in law practice demands that you relentlessly upgrade your skills.[1] Ironically, failure is a necessary ingredient of getting better. Any success book you ever read will tell you that you need to embrace failure. They will recount many success stories that were preceded with countless failures until the success was achieved. The same is true for law practice. Every step of the way, use negative client feedback, failures, bad decisions, and the fear of mistakes to educate you to do better. "A characteristic of high achievers is that they love doing new things, learning new skills, starting new projects. They are always searching for new techniques and methods to try."[2]

Listen to Clients

If you listen without being defensive, clients will help you get better. Years ago, I represented one of the most difficult, spoiled young women I have ever met. She used to call me every morning during my quiet time and give me hell. I would usually just take her call, wedge the phone between my chin and shoulder, and listen while I opened my mail. Somehow, she could sense I was opening my mail and she would shriek, "Are you looking at your mail?" I would say, "No." And she would say, "Oh yes you are, I can tell." Anyway, you get the point that this was the client from hell. Well, at the end of her representation, she chastised me for not telling her to change her will. She accused me of being guilty of malpractice. I explained that I was a divorce lawyer, not an estate lawyer. But her mind was unchanged. Well, even though this terrible, spoiled person had no credibility with me, I listened to her. I added a reminder about the necessity to change the will to my client intake checklist and my exit interview checklist.

Listen to Trusted Employees

The best barometer of firm performance is the opinion of trusted employees. Seek their opinion; involve them in decisions. If there is an employee problem, call them into your office and ask for their insights.

Learning from Experience

I do not think I have ever been to a trial where I did not come up with a list of about fifteen things I could have done better. This used to really bother me. Now I look forward to making this list. I actually have a special sheet of paper that I carry to hearings and trials and depositions which has the heading, "Things I Have Learned." On that sheet, I list everything that I think I could have done better, and I make note of a system or checklist I can create to make sure I improve.

Autopsy Without Blame

High performers in sports and other pursuits are experts at accepting criticism; they not only accept criticism, they embrace it.[3] Jim Collins's *Good to Great* coined the phrase "autopsy without blame."[4] This means that your organization should take a look at every situation that does not go well and analyze it—without blame—to see what happened and to learn how you can improve. If something happens in your office that is not right, do not go crazy and scream; instead conduct an autopsy without blame. Assemble your staff and say, "Now, we had an occurrence in the Smith case where our complaint was filed without a request for temporary alimony." Then ask, without judgment, "How did this happen?" Then put the all-important question to them: "What system can we put in place to make sure this does not happen again?"

Build Mistake Prevention into Forms and Procedures

Create checklists for every procedure that you perform, ranging from client intake to drafting pleadings, client interviews, setting up files, closing files, preparing for trial, and on and on. Build on and amend these checklists periodically.

Beware When Things Are Going Good

Experience has taught me that when I stop and reflect and say, "You know, everything is just the way I want it," something bad is about to happen; all hell is about to break loose. I was always concerned that such a belief was a bad attitude until I read that Walt Disney carried the following saying on the back of his business card which he kept in his wallet: "Just when everyone is saying how great you are is when you're the most vulnerable."[5] What this means is that even when things are going well, you must never stop learning and trying to get better.

Read

If you want to be great at what you do, you should be a voracious reader. You should read everything you can on operating a business, managing staff, being a success, client service, and so on.

Coaching

Every lawyer who is committed to success should hire a business coach. As you may know from reading this book, I have had several business coaches over the years. The most prominent in my business life, as I have already said, have been Atticus out of Orlando, Florida, and Jerry Schwartz out of Memphis, Tennessee. A good coach does not tell you how to do things; she holds up a mirror. A good coach asks questions, and you provide the answers. Think about it, Tiger Woods is the best golfer who ever lived. He knows how to play golf almost perfectly. He has set more records than anyone, ever, at his age. But Tiger Woods has a coach.

> For every recognized winner there is a coach in the background. Winners recognize that good coaches have knowledge and information beyond their own capabilities, and they are willing to assimilate this through the coach. They are open to the leadership of others. The great ones have mentors.[6]

Groups

Anyone who wants to be good at what he does gets together with others who do the same thing. The purpose is to exchange ideas, check yourself, confirm your own excellence, create connections. There are many groups lawyers can join. Start with the ABA Family Law Section and Law Practice Management Section. Join your state bar's family law section and its committees. If you wish to join other organizations, look around and see whom you admire. Ask them what groups they have joined and ask them if they would recommend you for membership.

Mastering Your Trade

Set about to master your trade. If you are going to dedicate your life to being a divorce lawyer, determine to become the best that you can be. As I have already pointed out, my experience with law and other professions tells me that mastering your trade takes a minimum of ten years. If you are a lawyer with fewer than ten years of experience, you can perform well but you are not a master. You simply cannot have the body of experience necessary to be a master. And you cannot become a master within ten years without supreme dedication of all your efforts and talents to the task.

Run Your Office Like a Dictator

When you start your own law practice, it is *your baby*. There is only one person who will pay for mistakes, and there is only one person who is exposed to liability, expense, and failure: YOU! Therefore, determine exactly how you want to do things and then do it that way. Let no one stop you. Let no one's criticism sidetrack you. Let no one saddle you with a lack of confidence. Create a vision and then go after it like George Patton on the way to Berlin with his tanks.

Take Quiet Time

Growth is always required. Allot time for innovating, experimenting, and dreaming.[7] Allow yourself quiet time:

> Yet all significant, long-lasting personal change must usually begin in a quiet space that promotes reflection, which in turn leads to self-awareness. You *must* withdraw from the hullabaloo of life from time to time to give yourself an opportunity to look within and explore those areas that need transforming.[8]

Additional Resources

For an excellent book on getting better and finding success, with practical worksheets, see Stedman Graham, *You Can Make It Happen* (New York: Simon & Schuster, 1997). For an excellent book on how to get better in times of change, see Robert J. Kriegel and Louis Patler, *If It Ain't Broke—Break It* (New York: Warner Books, 1971).

Notes

1. Stolitz, Paul G., *Adversity Quotient*, p. 171 (New York: John Wiley & Sons, 1997).

2. Murphy, Shane, *The Achievement Zone*, p. 202 (New York: Berkley Books, 1996).

3. Ibid., p. 178.

4. Collins, Jim, *Good to Great*, p. 77 (New York: HarperCollins, 2001).

5. Connellan, Tom, *Inside the Magic Kingdom*, p. 13 (Austin, TX: Bard Press, 1997).

6. Coonradt, Charles A., *The Game of Work*, p. 109 (Park City UT: The Game of Work, 1991).

7. Charan, Ram, and Noel Tichy, *Every Business Is a Growth Business*, p. 169 (New York: Random House, 1998).

8. Benson, Herbert, and William Proctor, *The Break-out Principle*, p. 106 (New York: Scribner, 2003).

Taking Care of Yourself 20

Y OU—YOUR MIND, YOUR BODY, YOUR SPIRIT—are your production engine. You must take care of yourself so that you can perform at peak capacity over the long haul. Your body cannot be traded in for a new model, and your performance is largely dependent on good health.[1] Lawyers are notorious for working their butts off and neglecting themselves. As a group they suffer from a very high incidence of depression and alcoholism. In Mississippi alone, there have been an alarming number of suicides among lawyers and judges. These suicides were caused, in my opinion, by a mismanagement of the production engine: the lawyer himself. You must construct a practice and personal habits that lead to a healthy you. View your body as an Indy 500 racing machine, designed to run at peak performance over long distances. Take care of your body, the same way they take care of the Indy 500 race car. Lawyers must be particularly vigilant of their health and their "mind, body, and spirit."

Seek Balance

I tell people that life is like that gopher pop-up game. You know, the one where there are a bunch of gopher holes and you have a big mallet and the object is to hit a gopher on the head just as soon as he pops up. Well, imagine your life as having five gopher holes: one for your spouse, one for your children, one for your health, one for your profession, and one for your finances. The object of the game of life is to keep the gopher from popping up in any one of those holes. In other words, the object of life is to make sure that none of the essential areas of your life becomes a problem. Since we only have two hands (or one mallet), it is extremely hard to keep a life problem from popping up. And one thing we know for sure: if we spend too much time paying attention to one aspect of our lives, a gopher is going to pop up in another area. By the same token, if we do not focus enough on each area, a gopher is going to pop up somewhere. And when the proverbial gopher pops up in one area of our lives, all of the other areas are then in trouble too, are they not?

The way to keep as many of the gopher holes covered as possible is to practice balance. We simply cannot sacrifice any area of our lives in pursuit of another. The mistake lawyers make is that they think they must sacrifice all areas of their lives for their profession. This mentality starts in law school. I shall never forget that hot day in August of 1975 when I sat in orientation at the University of Mississippi. The first thing they told us was that to succeed "you have to marry the law." Then they told us to look at the people to the left and the right of us and said, "They won't be here when you are done." After law school, we meet the demands of superiors for billed hours. And when we start our own practice, we see every hour missed from work as dollars out of our pocket. This work ethic can lead to the attainment of skills, income, and distinction, but the price is failed home lives, depression, and alcoholism. Walt Bachman writes that one of the lessons he has learned in law practice that he was not taught in law school is that "10% of the lawyer's soul dies for every 100 hours worked in excess of 1600 per year."[2]

Do not get me wrong: a lawyer has to work hard and pay his dues to master his trade. In fact, it may be necessary to be a little "out of balance" in the first ten years of practice or when you are just starting your business. In *Rich Dad, Poor Dad*, Richard Kiyosaki states, "To make progress, you must first go unbalanced."[3] But some balance is appropriate and great care must be taken to pay the right amount of attention to each area of life, or it will pop up and bite you.

Diet

Watch your diet. Eat foods that provide energy; avoid foods that are acidic and detract from energy and performance. You should research this for yourself, but here are some suggestions.

Avoid caffeine. Avoid all caffeine, except a single cup of green tea in the morning. Caffeine has many deleterious effects. It is dangerous to blood pressure and contributes to hypertension. It can create sleep disturbance.

Avoid sugar. Avoid sugar, particularly refined sugar. It causes a brief and artificial high, which leads to severe energy drop in the long term. It also leads to weight gain.

Drink water. Every single health article you will ever read will extol the virtues of drinking a lot of water. Keep a cool glass of spring water on your desk.

Eat breakfast. Whenever you read any list of health tips, whether it is ten tips or seven, or whatever, you will see the recommendation of eating a good breakfast. All health literature says that your biggest meal should be your first. You have to put fuel in your tank before a trip. The same is true for your body.

Eat six times per day. According to health experts, the human body is designed to receive food six times a day, not three. This regimen is a difficult habit to follow, because everyone else eats only three times a day, but it will pay huge dividends in terms of maintaining your energy and will also help you reduce your weight, if done properly.

Eat fish and green vegetables. Did you ever get up from a meal of broiled fish and green vegetables and feel bad? NO. Eat as much of these foods as possible.

Snack on healthy foods. Snack on foods such as fruit and nuts.

Fitness

Divorce lawyers are warriors. We face human trial, suffering, and tragedy all day, every day. We deal with adversaries and judges who are trying to defeat everything we do. We should prepare ourselves for these trials and battles by being in "fighting shape." We should create daily habits that involve physical fitness. Working out the body physically creates a sense of well-being, elevates mental acuity, and relieves stress, among other things.[4] Lawyers need all of this, particularly in light of the statistics on the high percentages of lawyers with addiction and depression problems. Become a health fanatic. Hire a trainer. Set specific, physical development goals. If you do not wish to do this, all you have to do is walk every day for thirty minutes. The rest will follow.

Alcohol

Alcohol is a depressant. It is a dangerous commodity to lawyers for many reasons. It interferes with judgment, and it affects discipline and self-control. It can lead to depression. Lawyers are particularly susceptible to alcohol problems and must manage it carefully.

Depression

As a divorce lawyer, you witness a lot of human tragedy, immorality, and sadness every day. You must recognize that you are asking yourself to experience a higher dose of depressing situations than may be healthy. Observe yourself. Pay attention to the effects of your business on your body and your mind and your spirit. Look for mechanisms to relieve the stress and keep your spirits elevated. A number of tools can keep your spirit healthy, notably:

> *Work out.* A workout releases endorphins and other body chemicals that promote a sense of well-being.
>
> *Meditate.* Practice meditation and/or prayer every day for fifteen to thirty minutes. This quiet time will insulate you against the spiritual and emotional rigors of the day.
>
> *Take up hobbies.* Enmesh yourself in hobbies that give you a sense of fulfillment.
>
> *Engage in religious activity.* If you have a faith, practice it to the fullest. Become as involved in your faith as you can.
>
> *Prioritize family.* After faith, your next priority should be your family. If you put your family behind your business, the spiritual drain will ultimately defeat your business and professional life.
>
> *Take trips.* Over ten years ago, I realized that my practice never took me out of Mississippi. I joined the ABA Section of Family Law and made a personal commitment to travel to every meeting, three times per year. Attendance at the meetings provides me with a four-day trip every three months to a great location in the world. These trips are rejuvenating and exhilarating. They open the mind and create vitality.
>
> *Read books.* There is nothing better for the spirit and the mind than reading. Set aside time each day to read things that you enjoy.

Rest

For most of my life, the term *rest* was a dirty word. All of my training dictated that I had to work every possible minute, that I had to work so hard it "hurt." After all, "there is no gain without pain." At least that is what my football and wrestling and weightlifting coaches always told me. To a certain extent, it is true that there can be no gain without pain. But every good athlete should know that the body must be given time to rest, or it will not perform as well. The same is true for us lawyers. Give careful thought to making sure you are resting yourself properly. Here are some tips:

> *Get enough sleep.* Most people require seven to eight hours of sleep to be healthy. Create routines in your life that facilitate a proper night's sleep. If you really want to get into it, keep a "dream log" and write down your dreams. This will focus you on the importance of deep and restful sleep. For more insights into the benefits of sleep, see Elson M. Haas, M.D., *Staying Healthy with the Seasons* (Millbrae, CA: Celestial Arts, 1981).
>
> *Take time off.* Set aside time during the week to be away from work. Some management experts even advise that you take every third or fourth day off and that you spend the off day not doing *anything* pertaining to work. Do not even call the office. You may not be willing to take every third day off, or even an afternoon off per week, but maybe you can start by taking one weekday off per month. Use the day purely for yourself. Take care of errands. Go hiking. Play golf. Get your mind off of the office totally. Benjamin Sells, a lawyer turned psychotherapist, talks of the need of the soul for time:
>
> Soul requires real time, time that has room for pauses, and silence, and inactivity; time lingering like a summer afternoon, stretching lazily into evening without a care in the world, time to putter about, a day gone amidst odd jobs and piddly things.[5]
>
> The first day I took time off I felt guilty. I ended up playing golf with a young banker. That afternoon of golf led to the start of a friendship, and that banker ultimately loaned me the money for my first building. So the rest "paid off."

Rest during the day. We routinely push ourselves to concentrate for eight or more hours, straight. But the truth is that our minds and bodies are not made to do that. Our minds function best for no more than 90 to 120 minutes at a time. Experiment with resting every 90 minutes. You can do this in any one of a number of ways. You can close your eyes for five minutes; you can have a healthy snack; you can call a family member or walk down the hall of your office.

Notes

1. Waitley, Denis, *The Psychology of Winning* (New York: Berkley Publishing, 1974).

2. Bachman, Walt, *Law vs. Life*, p. 107 (New York: Four Directions Press, 1995).

3. Kiyosaki, Richard T., *Rich Dad, Poor Dad*, p. 137 (Paradise Valley, AZ: TechPress, 1997).

4. Murphy, Shane, *The Achievement Zone*, pp. 204–211 (New York: Berkley Books, 1996).

5. Sells, Benjamin, *The Soul of the Law*, p. 79 (Rockport, MA: Element, 1994).

Parting Thoughts 21

JUST AS YOU SHOULD CREATE A VISION for the look of
your firm over the years, you should also create a
vision for how and when and under what terms you
will *quit* or *exit* your firm. Creating a vision for exiting
your firm will help you take the proper steps along
the way to make the exit you envision a reality. If you
do not decide fairly soon how long you are going to
practice, the decision will be made for you, and that
decision will probably be "forever." Deciding on an
ending date for your practice of law will help you
focus on, and create a deadline for, accomplishing
what needs to be accomplished for you to retire. To
properly plan for your exit from practice, carefully
plan the kind of lifestyle you would like to have upon
retirement and the money necessary to achieve it.
Assistance with this type of planning can be obtained
from most financial planners. To assist you with this
type of analysis, see Appendix 21A, which provides an
exit plan worksheet authored by Atticus.

Justice

There are two basic methods by which judges apply justice. Both methods are akin to those we use to deal with our children. Imagine that you have two children and they are fighting in your kitchen. There are two basic ways you deal with it, and neither method involves extensive inquiry or getting to the truth. Both methods involve an impatient parent trying to get the children out of his way so he can do what he wants. The first method of dispute resolution is "the cookie method." This is where the parent cannot tell which child has the better claim to something, and not wanting either child to be unhappy, gives a cookie to each of them, even if only one of them is entitled to it. Here is how this method works: Dad says, "Here's a cookie for you and here's a cookie for you." Well, that is what judges do. They often do not know how to sort out who should get the cookie, but not wanting anyone to be mad, they give a cookie to both. The problem with this approach is that even though you might have gotten a satisfactory result, you are left with a bitter taste in your mouth at the injustice of the side in error getting a cookie too.

The second method is the "you go to your room and you go to your room method." This is where the parent cannot tell who is at fault in starting the fight, but is angry that a fight has broken out. In this method, the parent decides to punish both children despite an inkling as to which one started it. This method goes like this. Mom says: "You go to your room." Child says: "But Mom, she started it." Mom: "I don't care, go to your room." Then the other child says: "Ha Ha." Mom swats child two on the butt and sends her to her room too. Before you embark upon a discovery dispute, or strike out for court with high hopes of total victory because you have the law on your side, it is important for you to recognize the two basic methods of dispensing justice.

Cycles

It is weird, but things happen in groups and cycles. There is no rhyme or reason for it most of the time. Sometimes I look up and realize I am representing all kinds of doctors' wives. Sometimes I get a rash of calls from people who picked me out of the phone book. Sometimes we feel like everything is going our way. Sometimes we feel that the judges have something personal against us because we cannot seem to get what we want. Just this past month, I had several cases involving abuse in which temporary restraining orders were obtained. A few months ago, I had a rash of cases of clients causing me a great deal of grief. The moral of this story is to be careful before you decide a cycle is a trend. Usually, cycles do not mean anything.

The Horrible Result

If you are a litigator and you have not had a result that is a total disaster, you are a very rare bird. I suffered my first disaster in the very early years of my new business. I was aghast; I could not believe it. The result was totally unfair and not based on law or evidence. I will never forget gasping for air as I read the decision. I experienced months and months of regret and soul searching about my worth as a lawyer. Well, such a result has happened since. My experience is that I get "tagged" with one of these results every three years or so. The moral of this story is to expect a disaster every once in awhile and realize that it has nothing to do with you.

Three Accidents Together Cause a Disaster

I have fretted and fretted over the possibility that I would make a terrible mistake in a file that would cause an unjust result for my client. I used to worry terribly and lose sleep over the possibility of a single, simple mistake causing disaster. After years of worrying and having no disasters happen, even though I have made mistakes, I finally realized that a single mistake will rarely, if ever, cause a disaster. However, disaster is guaranteed when *three* unlikely mistakes come together, either through coincidence or bad luck or sloppiness. This means that we usually have at least two chances to avert disaster once a mistake is made. It means we should be alert at all times and leap to handle matters when the first mistake is made. It means we should create fail-safe measures to catch mistakes.

Here is an example of what I am talking about. I am always fearful of missing an answer due date. The first line of defense in this is my memory. But I know that my memory can be faulty, so I follow a procedure through which my paralegal is supposed to immediately calendar the due date upon receipt of the complaint. Finally, when we receive a complaint, we immediately file a pleading that I have designed called "Entry of Appearance, Motion for Extension of Time and General Denial." This pleading is designed only to place the other side under an obligation to send me written notice before attempting to obtain a default. So you see, there are three lines of protection. This is the way NASA averts disaster. Look for ways to create at least three systems to protect you in every endeavor.

When You Can't Lose

If you ever think you have a case or position that you feel is so strong that you cannot lose, watch out. If you ever feel that way, become suspicious. Carefully double check your law or facts. Carefully reconsider the qualities of your opponent or your judge. Prepare yourself and your client for a less than perfect result by saying something like, "I feel we have good facts and the law on our side, but going to court is always a gamble and there is no sure result."

We Did It All

About a year ago, I was meeting with my associate lamenting the fact that it seemed we had no business to work on. I was worried and wondered out loud, "What are we doing wrong, we don't have any business. What do you think happened to our business?" My associate thought for a second and calmly said, "There's nothing wrong; we just did all the work." I thought for a second and then chuckled, "You're right." There was nothing wrong with our business; we had simply completed all of the work and projects at about the same time.

Keep Journals on Your Business

Many books and professional coaches advocate keeping a journal. Keeping a journal causes you to stop and reflect on what you have done and what you want to do; in other words, it keeps you focused. Journaling also helps you sort out and isolate fears. Fears have a tendency to fly around in our heads. When we write, we tie those loose thoughts down. Journaling is also good for your mind, body, and spirit. Writing down your feelings has a positive effect on your immune system. "Expressing feelings in writing creates chemical changes in your body, resulting in better health."[1] One caveat on keeping a journal: Be careful what you record for others to see.

Conclusion

Building and successfully managing your own family law practice can be one of the most satisfying and fulfilling of all of your life experiences. The successfully managed family law practice will provide professional challenge and satisfaction; it can provide a comfortable living for you and your family; and it can permit manifold contributions to society. Successfully managing your family law practice allows you to change people's lives for the better. Family lawyers play a most important role in guiding families through their most difficult times. Successfully managing your practice also provides income and healthy workplaces for partners, employees, and their families.

Take the time to write a personal mission statement using the worksheets on the compact disk included with this book. Then create a business mission statement that serves your personal mission and goals. Finally, create concrete goals for your firm.

Everything else will flow from there. Good luck. Stay healthy and enjoy the process of getting better every day!

Note

1. Stolitz, Paul G., *Adversity Quotient*, p. 77 (New York: John Wiley & Sons, 1997).

Index

List of Appendices

The Appendices listed below are included on the accompanying CD-ROM. The file formats allow you to easily read and customize the material to your needs. For additional information, terms, and conditions pertaining to the files on the CD-ROM, please open and read the "readme.doc" file on the CD-ROM.

Additional Resources from the American Bar Association

101+ Practical Solutions for the Family Lawyer: Sensible Answers to Common Problems, Second Edition, by Gregg Herman, 2003

The 1040 Handbook: A Guide to Income and Discovery, Fourth Edition, by Jack Zuckerman, Emily M. Reich, William F. Wolf, Peggy L. Podell, and David M. Franklin, 2003

Assisted Reproductive Technology: A Lawyer's Guide to Emerging Law and Science, by Charles P. Kindregan, Jr., and Maureen McBrien, 2006

Attacking and Defending Marital Agreements, by Laura W. Morgan and Brett R. Turner, 2001

Balancing Competing Interests in Family Law, Second Edition, by John C. Mayoue, 2003

The Business Tax Return Handbook, Second Edition, by Jack Zuckerman and William F. Wolf, 2004

Child Sexual Abuse in Civil Cases: A Guide to Custody and Tort Actions, by Ann M. Haralambie, 1999

Children Held Hostage: Dealing with Programmed and Brainwashed Children, by Stanley S. Clawar and Brynne V. Rivlin, 1991

Client Manual: FAQs: Frequently Asked Questions About Divorce (*Family Advocate* magazine), July 2005

Client Manual: My Parents Are Getting Divorced (*Family Advocate* magazine), July 2006

Collaborative Law: Achieving Effective Resolution in Divorce without Litigation, by Pauline H. Tesler, 2001

Collecting Your Fee: Getting Paid from Intake to Invoice, by Edward Poll, 2002

The Complete QDRO Handbook: Dividing ERISA, Military, and Civil Service Pensions and Collecting Child Support from Employee Benefit Plans, by David Clayton Carrad, 2004

Creating Effective Parenting Plans: A Developmental Approach for Lawyers and Divorce Professionals, by John Hartson and Brenda Payne, 2006

The Divorce Trial Manual: From Initial Interview to Closing Argument, by Lynne Z. Gold-Bikin and Stephen Kolodny, 2003

The Essential Formbook: Comprehensive Management Tools for Lawyers, Vols. I-IV, by Gary A. Munneke and Anthony C. Davis, 2003–2006

Flying Solo: A Survival Guide for the Solo and Small Firm Lawyer, Fourth Edition, edited by K. William Gibson, 2005

How to Capture and Keep Clients: Marketing Strategies for Lawyers, edited by Jennifer Rose, 2005

How to Start & Build a Law Practice, Fifth Edition, by Jay G. Foonberg, 2004

Law Office Procedures Manual for Solos and Small Firms, Third Edition, by Demetrios Dimitriou, 2005

The Lawyer's Business Valuation Handbook: Understanding Financial Statements, Appraisal Reports, and Expert Testimony, by Shannon P. Pratt, 2000

The Lawyer's Guide to Adobe® Acrobat®, Second Edition, by David L. Masters, 2005

The Lawyer's Guide to Creating a Business Plan (software package), by Linda Pinson, 2006

The Lawyer's Guide to Effective Yellow Pages Advertising, Second Edition, by Kerry Randall and Andru J. Johnson, 2005

The Lawyer's Guide to Fact Finding on the Internet, Third Edition, by Carole A. Levitt and Mark E. Rosch, 2006

The Lawyer's Guide to Increasing Revenue, by Arthur G. Greene, 2005

The Lawyer's Guide to Marketing Your Practice, Second Edition, edited by James A. Durham and Deborah McMurray, 2004

The Lawyer's Guide to Strategic Planning, by Thomas C. Grella and Michael L. Hudkins, 2004

Letters for Lawyers: Essential Communications for Clients, Prospects, and Others, Second Edition, by Thomas E. Kane

The Military Divorce Handbook: A Practical Guide to Representing Military Personnel and Their Families, by Mark E. Sullivan, 2006

The Successful Lawyer: Powerful Strategies to Transform Your Practice (book and audio CDs), by Gerald A. Riskin, 2005

Through the Client's Eyes, Second Edition, by Henry W. Ewalt, 2002